BANK BUILDERS

BANK BUILDERS

EDWIN HEATHCOTE

WILEY-ACADEMY

Acknowledgements

I would first like to thank my wife Krisztina who tolerates me being a writer and even encourages me. I would like to point out that no banks sponsored or assisted in the publication of this book. I extend my thanks to John McAslan, the Bank of England Archive and David Cook. I would also like to thank Mario Bettella and Andrea Bettella, Francesca Wisniewska and Francesca Ciurlante at Artmedia who designed the book and Maggie Toy and Mariangela Palazzi-Williams without whom the book would not have appeared at all.

Photographic credits

All photographs are courtesy of the architects or from the Architectural Press archive, unless stated otherwise; every effort has been made to locate sources and credit material but in the very few cases where this has not been possible our apologies are extended: Sir John Soane's Museum. pg 10, Bank of England Archives pg 15, Stefan Buzan pg 55, Timothy Hursley pps 62, 63, 64, 66,67, 200, Richard Bryant pg 65, Christian Kandzia pps 68-77, Alo Zanetta pps 84, 86, 89, Pino Musi pps 87, 88, 89 (bottom pair), 90-92, Enrico Cano pps 93-95, S. Couturier pps 96, 98, 99 (bottom), 101 (top), B. Cornette pps 97, 99, G. Fessy pps 100-101, Christian Richters pps 108, 115, Ian Lambert pps 132, 134, 135,136, 138 (top), Joshua White pps 142-145, Whit Preston pg 144, Peter Cook pps 166, 172, Misao Suzuki pps 181-182, Catala Roca pps 178, 180, Katsuyoshi Savada pps 192-197, T. Duda pps 204, 206.

Cover: Old Broad Street, EPR
Frontispiece: Landesgirokasse, Stuttgart, Günter Behnisch
Page 6: Banque Bruxelles Lambert, Mario Botta

First published in Great Britain in 2000 by
WILEY-ACADEMY

A division of
JOHN WILEY & SONS
Baffins Lane
Chichester
West Sussex PO19 1UD

ISBN: 0-471-853-593

Other Wiley Editorial Offices
New York • Weinheim • Brisbane • Singapore • Toronto

Printed and bound in Italy

CONTENTS

PREFACE

The bank is one of the key buildings in the city; its position and status is comparable to that of the theatre, the church, the station, the town hall or any of the other buildings around which our lives revolve, even if we are unaccustomed to think in that way. Banks occupy a pivotal place in our lives, decisions will be taken within their walls which affect our lives individually and collectively. The banks are aware of their importance and have traditionally sought to create an image of stability, solidity and permanence through built form which is why they tend to remain with us for longer than the more ephemeral high street shops and businesses. To some extent this situation has been changing over recent years.

The banks themselves are portraying their business more as a service than as a fundamental cornerstone of our existence; a position which is increasingly seen as too arrogant and distant for our service-sector culture. As branches and small banks begin to reorganise into money shops rather than the semi-sacred space of their grander predecessors, the banks' headquarter buildings become the flagship and a recognisable presence in the cities and take on ever more importance.

Both trends can be seen to have their roots firmly in the past. The bank began as a money-shop, or rather booth, a moveable market stand designed to attract as little undesirable attention as possible behind which a money changer would operate to facilitate the buying and selling of goods in different currencies. A little later the great banking families of Florence built their palaces on prominent city centres sites and created an architecture which spoke eloquently of wealth and power and of the bank's power to literally buy the centre of the mercantile city if it so wished. Unlike the booths of the money changers, this architecture was unafraid to show off wealth but at the same time displayed an architectural strength and impenetrability which eliminated the need for a *keep out* sign. In these two early types we have the germ of all banks, of all the branches and the headquarters buildings. The history of bank architecture is the history of the attempts of architects to reconcile these two archetypes, the mobile and open market stall and the severe and forbidding fortress. Add to these the notion of the exchange, itself a blend of the market-square which developed into the courtyard type of the early exchanges, and the coffee-house where so much of the actual speculation and business occurred, and we have the basis for the development of the modern bank.

In this book I have attempted to bring together a broad cross-section of recent bank architecture in order to examine how these archetypes have thrived and survived in built form and how they are interpreted by some of the best and most successful modern architects. I have also written an introduction in which I try to very briefly outline the history of bank and exchange architecture in the Western tradition to form a context for the modern buildings that follow. Between the two sections I have included short chapters on a few architects who fundamentally altered the architecture of finance at the outset of the twentieth century and whose effects is still felt powerfully by all those designing in the field.

This book is not intended as a complete work of reference, there are many fine buildings which have been left out and a number of rather poor buildings which have been included, because they are representative of what is being built by banks today. Most of the buildings featured in this volume are headquarters buildings and there could be some criticism levelled at me that these are really no more than office blocks and have little to do with a specific architecture of banking. I would argue that this is not the case that it is precisely in the headquarters buildings that the banks are doing what the Medici did before them in Florence: that is creating an image of wealth, responsibility, power and stability. Also, of course, it is in these showpiece buildings that the banks can illustrate their commitment to design and architecture by commissioning a major building and it may well be one of the very few opportunities an architect will have to show what can be done on a big city-centre site with a big budget. Most architects around the world, despite complaining of lack of budget and opportunities elsewhere, still manage to create dull buildings given these generous circumstances.

It is precisely because of the often dire quality of bank buildings which have tended to irrevocably ruin many city-centres in the post-war years, that I hope that this book will stimulate thought and debate about what constitutes bank architecture and how the subject can be addressed by architects and clients in the wake of the massive and visible failure of so many of their immediate predecessors. I hope this selection of buildings will help the banks, the architects, the people who work in these buildings and the people who have to live around them to think about a subject which has hitherto been sparsely documented and virtually ignored by architectural historians and writers.

Edwin Heathcote

INTRODUCTION

Heinrich Heine once said that money is the religion of modernity. In the century and a half which has followed his death, the prescience of this statement has been powerfully reinforced. At the beginning of the twenty-first century money has become ensconced as the greatest and most universal of religions and its churches are the banks. The Gothic cathedrals, the wonders of medieval Europe, were erected in an intense burst of faith, confidence and will aided by great leaps in technical knowledge and architectural invention. The cathedrals of the modern world have been constructed by organisations even more wide reaching in power and influence than the medieval Church. Ironically, they rely equally on faith for their continuing existence and prosperity; that tremendous and all-important faith now goes under the name of credit.

The power of the banks is immeasurable and modern technocratic societies would collapse instantaneously without them. They are the true market places and urban centres of the modern city, perhaps analogous in this way as well to the churches which formed the nucleus of the city of the Middle Ages. But just as the invention of the flying buttress allowed Gothic architecture to achieve the lofty ideals of its builders and the butterfly-wing delicacy of its stonework by eliminating all but the essential structural elements, so computer and information technology have radically changed the functional needs of bank architecture to the extent that transactions can now take place through terminals in the wall. Technology has freed bank architecture from its traditional role: huge, imposing halls have been replaced by banking suites and tellers behind computer screens, rather than behind counters; back-rooms full of clerks have been replaced by telephone banking centres in anonymous out-of-town locations; bustling, high maintenance dealing floors at the heart of the city

by traders at terminals in lower rent offices on the outskirts. Yet just as the cathedral builders sought to express faith in their system by building into the sky, so modern bank headquarters need to express the unassailable power, the wealth and the security of the firms which inhabit them.

As such, the architecture of the banks has come to parallel the creation of the cathedrals as an expression of the *Zeitgeist* of a modern society which aspires to, and is built upon, money above all else. The weekly sermons which we all listen to now come no longer from the darkened pulpit but from a television screen showing a reporter against a background of busy traders, flickering monitors and an expanse of open-plan office floor. The pronouncements which truly affect our lives are the latest changes in interest rates, movements in share indices and currencies. Decisions taken in bank boardrooms control the engines of the international economy determining whether we still have a job the following day, fractions of percentage points can make the difference between being able to repay a loan or mortgage and bankruptcy. Yet the settings of these momentous decisions remain curiously anonymous. Like the obscure language of the international economic markets, these buildings seem to shelter a privileged clique of decision makers, a world which can seem intimidating, arrogant and distant. The scuttling figures that form the background to economic news reports with their famously grand salaries, cynically and memorably described by Tom Wolfe as 'Masters of the Universe', seem to exist in a different, rarified sphere. It has traditionally been the task (although it may be argued that this is now changing) of the architects of the great banking institutions to maintain this image of lofty seclusion, of power, of stability and of separateness from those who remain outside this privileged world. The history of an architecture which first attempts to express these ideas has its roots in Renaissance Italy, which is where any analysis of this building type must begin.

THE ARCHITECTURE OF MONEY – THE BEGINNINGS OF BANKING

It is hard to trace the origins of banking as so much depends on the definition of the term. However, it seems that rudimentary forms of lending and deposit, at rates of interest, were already available from the temples and royal treasuries of Mesopotamia built at the very beginning of Western civilisation in the third millennium BC. The ancient Greeks developed strongholds which were used for the safe storage of valuables in an age of war and insecurity while the rise of the Roman Empire witnessed the dawn of money shops which fulfilled many of the roles of the modern bank, where citizens could change money, give loans or take deposits. The Roman period also saw the beginnings of a laicisation of banking. Where earlier empires and civilisations had been characterised by the close control of any semblance of banking by the priesthood, with the temple treasuries acting as repositories and the minting of money also often occurring under priestly supervision, the Roman Empire spawned the beginnings of a secular system. The huge size of the empire and the complexity of the collection of taxes and tribute from around the various provinces necessitated the development of a network of what could now be recognised as banks and surprisingly international credit businesses, all of which were privately owned. The collapse of the Roman Empire brought an abrupt end to these developments and it was not until the medieval period that anything like a comparable system began to emerge.

The crusades from the eleventh century onwards proved to be a critical factor in the revival of a form of international banking. Hugely expensive and covering a number of countries and kingdoms each with their own currency, the adventures of the crusades were financed by kings, wealthy nobles and, of course, by the Church. It became necessary to create an international system of credit to enable the crusades to continue and thus it was during the period of the crusades (1095-1204) that the Italian city states became established as centres of this international financing. The Italian cities were conveniently situated in the Mediterranean as the embarkation point for journeys to the Middle East and had already established a network of far-reaching trading and cultural links. The northern Italians, in particular, were so successful in the emerging financial markets that the term 'Lombards' remained synonymous with banking, for centuries after; indeed Lombard Street in the City of London has been the epicentre of the British banking world since the fourteenth century. The Lombards had replaced the Jews as the controllers of international finance. For centuries the Jews had a virtual monopoly on the money-lending business which was often more a branch of pawnbroking than what we would recognise as banking today. Charlemagne (742-814) had found the Jews with their international family connections indispensable in building up international trade and diplomacy and they maintained this privileged position of financial supremacy until the rise of anti-semitism in medieval Europe which resulted in expulsions, pogroms and anti-Jewish legislation. Ironically, the anti-Jewish laws often helped to maintain Jewish domination of local financial operations and money lending. Jews found themselves unable to find employment outside their own community or within the established guild systems and the private operations of pawnbroking and moneylending alone remained open to them. Christian censure of usury also favoured the Jews (although Moses himself

Two views of Soane's Bank of England in ruins, rendered by J Gandy
TOP: The Rotunda in ruins, 1798; BOTTOM: Bird's eye view, 1830

had pronounced against the charging of interest on loans) so it was again ironic that the Lombards reached their position of unassailable financial domination of medieval Europe through their role as the collectors of the Papal taxes known as Peter's Pence. The collection of these revenues involved a great deal of money-changing as taxes came from across Western Europe and it was in the field of moneychanging that the beginnings of an international credit system began to evolve. The emergence of a semblance of international finance was made inevitable by the huge markets of medieval France and of Champagne in particular. The range and truly international provenance of the goods at these fairs meant that money changing and credit were at the heart of activities and these markets gave rise for the first time to the large-scale replacement of trading using money, with goods being bought and sold using only bills of exchange. It was the dawn of international banking.

Besides the Lombards and the Jews the other crucial players in the development of international finance had been the often hugely wealthy monastic orders and later the Knights Templar. The Templars were founded by a group of French knights in Jerusalem in the early twelfth century and were instrumental in implementing the crusades. Their full name, 'Poor Knights of Christ and of the Temple of Solomon', and the fact that members swore an oath of poverty makes it seem almost absurd that this order should have become the single most powerful and influential force in the finances of thirteenth-century Europe. Together the wealth of the monastic orders and the Templars was responsible for the building boom of the medieval age – the great cathedrals remain as testimony to their efforts. Indeed so successful were the Templars in their financial activities that an envious Pope Clement V and Philip IV of France, also known as Philip the Fair, were moved to destroy the order in 1307 and seize its riches. The motives of brotherhood (in a masonic rather than familial sense) and Christianity together with the sense of community which drove the Templars gave way to the development and rise to prominence of the idea of the individual in a late medieval Italy on the brink of the Renaissance. This coincided with the emergence of individuals and families as the driving force in banking.

At this stage there was no architecture of banking, in fact the nature of business had demanded a versatility and mobility which precluded the possibility of a per-manent architectural setting. In the most literal way the Lombards conducted their business in money markets on modest market stalls and timber counters. The word *bank* shares its roots with the Italian word *banca* which can mean desk, bench, counter, stall or the bank itself. If a trader became insolvent his stall was smashed up, the Italian phrase for this, *banca rotta* (*rotta* being 'break'), has filtered down to us as the word *bankrupt*. The origin of the word describes precisely the nature of early banking; usually a man working from behind a portable timber counter or table. The portability was crucial to allow the stall to be set up around the circuit of markets, but the inconspicuous and unpretentious nature of a simple piece of furniture was also impor-tant as early banking business was conducted in such a way as not to attract attention. A precaution against envy, particularly in the case of the Jews, this was also an attempt not to call attention to the money; the early bankers naturally feared robbery and murder, neither of which was rare in the brutal world of medieval commerce. The end of the medieval period, however, ushered in new attitudes to banking and finance and witnessed the emergence of a new class of bankers who can be said to have bankrolled the Renaissance. It is at this point that a complex and highly sophisticated banking system began to emerge throughout Europe, one which remained unequalled until the nineteenth century, and it is at this point too that an architectural expression of the world of banking begins to appear.

The architecture of banking divided into two sepa-rate strands at the end of the medieval period. In the years of the late fourteenth century the great exchanges, the first significant buildings to be designed specifically to house banking business, were built. In 1382 the Loggia dei Mercanti was designed for Bologna and the following year an exchange was built in Barcelona, the Taula di Canvi. Other cities followed by providing early merchant bankers with venues for their work, Perpignan in 1397, Palma in 1426 and Valencia in 1483. In the following century, as the impetus of trade began to move north of the Alps, exchanges were built in Antwerp in 1531 and London in 1571. These buildings tended to be relatively simple structures, a blend of market hall and guildhall, usually a single large space with or without aisles, the demands on which have not changed considerably since their inception. But the most dramatic buildings were not the exchanges but the private houses and

TOP: Money changer, sixteenth century print, Germany
CENTRE: Palazzo Medici-Riccardi, Florence
BOTTOM: Palazzo Strozzi, Florence

palaces of the great banking dynasties. It is by looking at these that we begin to get an idea of the architectural expression of money. Venice and Genoa had been the two great centres of merchant banking but by the fifteenth century the focus had shifted firmly to Florence and it was against the complex and Machiavellian background of Florentine politics and trade that modern banking began to develop. Based largely on success in the textile and wool industries and boosted by the early adoption of double-entry book-keeping, fifteenth-century Florence was dominated by a few families who controlled the guilds, the city's trade and its finance. The most powerful of these families had agents in London and Bruges, the other centres of the international textile markets, as well as in the other Italian cities. A good illustration of the power of these dynasties came in 1433 when Cosimo de Medici was expelled from Florence in the aftermath of a political upset. He took the Medici bank with him to Venice and Florence was subsequently so devastated by the loss of trade and status incurred that the following year the city welcomed him back. After this episode, Cosimo de Medici effectively became the city's undisputed ruler.

The wealth amassed by the great banking families gave rise to envy and distrust; frequent riots were the only means of expression open to the city's oppressed masses and it was these volatile social conditions which gave rise to the appearance of the palaces of the banking families. Like the Romans, the Florentines lived above the shop. Their palaces were also their counting-houses, their strongholds and their offices and this model proved an enduring one, lasting recognisably into the nineteenth century. The palace had to fulfil a number of functions and its appearance had to make clear what these functions were. Firstly, there was to be no doubt that this was the house of a rich family, a family which was able to buy a piece of the city, in the best part of the city, and make it their own, a permanent presence in the urban landscape. Secondly, the building had to look forbidding enough and strong enough to deter any ideas of thievery or penetration. Cosimo de Medici's own Palazzo Medici-Riccardi, designed by Michelozzo and begun in 1444, provides perhaps the most perfect example of the type. An immense single block, the palace presents an austere and forbidding mass to the street. The ground floor is heavily rusticated, even the arches seem unable to penetrate the mass of the walls and when the building is finally entered through its roughly central door, the visitor is led through a dark, tunnel-like corridor; the effect is of passing through a single, massive wall. At the other end of the tunnel the visitor is greeted by a light, arcaded courtyard, based on Brunelleschi's nearby Foundling Hospital (1419-24), perhaps the finest of the early Renaissance buildings. It seems certain that one of the rooms was used as a strong-room and contained the coffers of the bank and that there was some accommodation for clerks, but other than this there was little separation between the worlds of business and leisure. The banking could have been conducted in any of the impressive rooms of the palace, consequently, although positioned at the beginning of an architecture to express the power of money and the status of the banker, the palace predates bank architecture. This said, the great Florentine palaces of the banking families remained perhaps the single most enduring influence on the architecture of finance for a half millennium after their completion. Other Florentine families followed by immortalising themselves in urban blocks; Giovanni Rucellai had his palace built (begun in 1446) by the master, Alberti, who revived for it the Roman tradition of the superimposition of the orders and Filippo Strozzi commissioned Il Cronaca to design his palace (begun in 1489). Although derived from the Medici palace, the Palazzo Strozzi presents a far more refined version of the style and, in direct competition, is far larger and more monumental. As well as these great milestones in urban architecture and self-aggrandisement it should also be remembered that the Renaissance itself was funded almost entirely by the banking dynasties. As well as virtually controlling the city, the Church was also a popular destination for a family keen to reinforce its hold over the affairs of state; in fact the Medicis produced no less than two popes – Leo X and Clement VII. In these positions of power, members of the banking families became the most important patrons of the arts, employing the great artists of the age from Brunelleschi to Raphael and Michelangelo. The role of bankers as patrons of the arts has remained an important one to this day; Florence was where it all started.

THE ASCENDENCE OF THE NORTH

The centre of the developing banking world had moved around from Venice to Genoa and then to Florence where the most sophisticated system was built up during the fifteenth century, but during the next century the impetus was to move once more, this time north of the Alps. Early banking was a perilous business, great fortunes were amassed but it proved far easier to lose them than to make them. The most lucrative loans were made to rulers, to kings to enable them to fight wars; backing the wrong horse could prove expensive and rulers frequently reneged on deals. Due to a series of costly miscalculations the Florentines began to lose their position at the pinnacle of international banking and the emergent nation states of Northern Europe, with the backing of wealthy governments, began to come to the forefront of the banking world. Bruges, the centre of the wool and textile trades, was the first Northern capital to eclipse the Italian city states. Here the bankers, together with other merchants, conducted their business in a square in front of the house of the van der Beursse family, thus giving the French language the word *bourse*, and the German *Börse*, or exchange. The Place de la Bourse was a public square surrounded by the premises of traders grouped by nations or state which were known as factories, or offices of factors, these latter being agents. When the constantly moving focus of European trade began shifting towards Antwerp, the city commissioned an exchange (in 1531) to meet the needs of trade and banking. Influenced more by the open-air atmosphere of the Place de la Bourse than by the enclosed exchanges of a century earlier in Spain, the attractive late Gothic building, designed by Dominicus van Waghemakere, took the form of a large, arcaded courtyard. Antwerp's primacy in the banking world also proved short lived ending when the Spanish conquered it in 1585. The focus moved further north again, to Amsterdam. Amsterdam was already in a good position for trade; the city had become the European centre for shipping, international trade and commerce, new colonies favouring the Atlantic and North Sea ports rather than the Mediterranean which had hitherto had supremacy. The city's impressive exchange (1608-11), designed by Hendrik de Keyser, was similar to the Antwerp exchange as it was based around a grand arcaded courtyard. Its construction consolidated Amsterdam's position as a leading banking city and its status was simultaneously confirmed beyond doubt by the success of the Wisselbank, founded in 1609. Europe had seen secular public banks before, the Banco della Piazza di

Rialto in Venice and the Banco di Santo Spirito (the Papal bank) had both been founded towards the end of the sixteenth century while the first such bank in northern Europe had been built in Rotterdam in 1599. The Wisselbank, however, proved to be in a different league. The Wisselbank (or exchange bank) was able to fund the rise of the city and the state in a co-ordinated and organised manner which was still alien to the rest of Europe. Huge loans to the phenomenally successful Dutch East India Company and investment into Amsterdam's infrastructure gave good returns. The bank was also able to give loans to the state as well as taking on the responsibility for minting coins. The Wisselbank also began to lend to private clients and by the end of the seventeenth century all large payments had to pass through it and thus all the major finance houses needed to hold accounts with the Wisselbank. Although Amsterdam was in the vanguard of the new relationship between state, city and bank and was taking full advantage of the stability which it gave to the country's powerful economy, the full potential of the system was to be realised in another fast-emerging Northern European capital, London.

The British had been looking enviously at the successes of the Dutch in trade and finance. The London Royal Exchange had been founded in 1566, well before that in Amsterdam, although its architecture was essentially of the same type, namely a building surrounding a large arcaded courtyard. Private banking in England was already well advanced by the seventeenth century with the great bankers emerging from the ranks of the goldsmiths' guild which had virtually monopolised the field. However, the confluence of a number of factors in the second half of the seventeenth century led to the establishment of the Bank of England which would see London firmly entrenched as the financial capital of Europe. The Great Fire of London in 1666 had provided the opportunity for a wholesale rebuilding of the city. This included a new exchange (1667-71) which was designed by Edward Jarman and also based on the courtyard model. Other factors included the accession to the throne of William and Mary in 1688. William of Orange was a Dutch king and remained chief magistrate of the United Provinces. In this capacity he was keen to help his fellow countrymen in their war against the French. A climate was created in which banking flourished as the Dutch and the British came together to defeat the threat of Louis

XIV's France; loans to governments were far more secure than those backed by the word of an absolute monarch and banking in Holland and England became more stable and institutionalised than it could ever have been in the turbulent political worlds of the Mediterranean countries. The Bank of England was founded in 1694 and it grew rapidly becoming the banker for the British government as well as fulfilling the role of a commercial bank and issuing its own bank notes (following on the success of paper money which had been introduced by the Bank of Stockholm in 1656). For the first forty years of its existence the Bank of England rented premises in London but it soon outgrew its limited accommodation. The bank responsible for managing the national debt and keeping government accounts was deemed to deserve a purpose-built structure and the site of the house of Sir John Houblon, then the governor of the bank, was chosen. An architectural competition was held and the bank was completed in 1734 to the designs of George Sampson. Sampson's building represents the real beginning of the history of bank architecture, yet it was a curious start. The original domestic use of the site provided a plan which was deep and narrow. As a result the new building resembled a private dwelling but behind the elegant Palladian facade lay a series of secure spaces including the Pay Hall, where members of the public conducted their transactions with the bank, and a courtyard to the rear of the building around which were arranged the private offices of the bank. In a curious way the deep site suited the purposes of the bank as it allowed a series of internal light-wells to be used for illuminating the rooms, a far safer solution than windows opening to public streets. The bank quickly outgrew its site and the next major step in its development consisted of a series of major extensions to the building by the architect Sir Robert Taylor. These included a large, domed rotunda, apparently based on the design of the Pantheon in Rome, around which four vaulted halls were built, each named after its function. The next phase of Taylor's work, the Court Room, is the only part of his design which has substantially survived, and even that has been moved and reconstructed although it still fulfils its original function today. In a wonderful demonstration of Heine's dictum about money being the religion of modernity St Christopher-le-Stocks, the church which had stood beside the bank, was demolished in1782 and the site was acquired by the bank. The reason for the church's demolition was that it posed a threat to the security of the site, a fact which was driven home by the Gordon Riots of 1780 which saw the bank besieged by a mob of protesters. The final stage of Taylor's work comprised the exquisitely subtle domed space of the Reduced Annuity Office, which, in its stripped and austere elegance, began to anticipate the work of Taylor's successor, Sir John Soane. Soane's work at the Bank of England would become perhaps the most admired and influential masterpiece of architecture in the banking world.

His virtual rebuilding of the Bank of England between 1788 and 1823 was pivotal in defining the architectural language of banking. Drawing inspiration from the great domed halls of the Romans, as Taylor had done earlier, Soane's new halls were theatrical and symbolic rather than purely functional. The purpose of these spaces was, like the Florentine palaces of the first banking dynasties, to stamp the bank's authority on the city and to overwhelm the visitor with their grandeur and ambition. Like the cavernous, awe inspiring interior landscapes of Piranesi, whose work was so influential upon Soane, these rooms were designed on the gargantuan scale of the newly fashionable ruins of Rome and the recently discovered ruins of Pompeii and Herculaneum. In fact the most striking drawing of Soane's Bank of England is that by Soane's favourite draughtsman, J M Gandy, who depicted the bank as a set of grand ruins, a method which allowed him to show a cut-away of the workings of this complex building but which, much more than being a graphic technique, represented the bank as a ruin to be marvelled at in the future, a sight to equal the remains of Rome. Soane employed a blend of the stripped Classical language with a monumental, almost Byzantine approach to mass and space which echoed the might of the buildings of the ancients rather than the palaces of the Renaissance. The size and depth of the site meant that the internal spaces were illuminated by glazed domes and lanterns with glazed arches between the ceiling vaults. Rotundas, Greek-cross plans and complex networks of vaulting and arches gave the building an air of temple-like grandeur. The bank was surrounded by a daunting, windowless perimeter wall designed to create the image of an impenetrable mass of stone. Heavy horizontal rustication emphasised the sheer length of the walls while

TOP: John Soane, The Bank of England, The London Office, 1798-99
BOTTOM: The Bank Stock Office, 1792-93

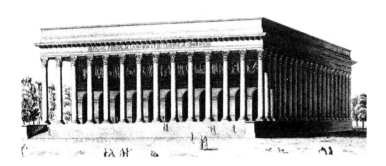

niches and set-backs (blank walls fronted with heavy colonnades) constantly reminded the viewer of the massive depth of the walls, which was of course an illusion, an architectural trick. The narrow slot of an entrance further reinforced the notion of solid impregnability.

Whilst the spaces within the bank were functional, well-lit and rational, their scale and monumentality were purely for effect. The building was made to impress. Despite the Byzantine feel of the structure, the interiors were characterised by a lightness and a denial of weight and mass. The lack of columns allowed a free flow of space with uninterrupted views and passage of light. Soane's bank was certainly the finest in the world at the time of construction and it remained unparalleled for a long time; perhaps it is not an exaggeration to say that it may never be bettered. Unfortunately the building did not survive, extensive rebuilding of the bank in the period between the wars meant that Soane's masterpiece was all but obliterated and, although parts of the building survive and other parts have been rebuilt, it is hard to imagine the impact that this structure, covering three acres, must have had on Georgian London and on the international banking world. Soane's designs represented the creation of an archetype of bank design, a new architectonic language designed to express confidence in the solidity and permanence of a great banking institution. The architectural implication was that money would be safe in these magnificent domed vaults.

THE NINETEENTH CENTURY – THE GENESIS OF THE MODERN BANK

Soane's Bank of England bridged the period of dramatic transition between the eighteenth and nineteenth centuries. The French Revolution sent shock waves through the European establishment, it also led indirectly to the founding of the Banque Nationale de France. The Bank of England had been forced to expand partly as a result of the burgeoning government debt sustained by the massively expensive Napoleonic Wars. France herself had resisted setting up a national bank in the wake of the disastrous issuing of *assignats,* the paper money issued in vast quantities by the government under the influence of John Law. This led to gross inflation and ultimately to the collapse of the Banque Generale in 1720, only four years after its foundation. But there was much support for the estab-

*TOP: CN Ledoux, Caisse d'Escompte (design), 1788
CENTRE: AT Brongniart, Paris Bourse, 1808-26
BOTTOM: Thomas de Thomon, St Petersburg Exchange, 1804-16*

16 BANK BUILDERS

lishment of a national bank, and it was an idea which seemed to appeal greatly to the new generation of revolutionary architects who were instrumental in the creation of an *architecture parlante*, buildings which would speak of their function in an eloquent, universal, almost Platonic architectonic language. Claude-Nicolas Ledoux's design for the Caisse d'Escompte of 1788 presents a forbidding vision of a bank as Greek temple, a vision of permanence and solidity guarded by two curious sentry-boxes and set in an austere, arcaded square reminiscent of the enigmatic, shadowy town-scapes of Giorgio De Chirico's paintings. In fact the vision, scale and architectural language which Ledoux had formulated were realised most effectively not in France but in Russia. Thomas de Thomon, a French architect who seems to have studied under Ledoux and who settled in St Petersburg in 1790, designed the city's new Bourse (stock exchange) in 1804. Part of a monumental set piece, de Thomon's Bourse is one of the most complete and perfect examples of the Classical architecture of finance. It is raised on a stark plinth of granite and flanked by trees and a pair of columns at the water's edge which display carvings symbolising Russia's great rivers and which also acted as illuminated beacons towards the sea. The building's interior is defined by a single, hugely impressive tunnel-vault giving an aura of solidity, of a building carved out of rock; precisely the image needed to counteract the perception of a stock exchange as a place of wild fluctuation and instability. It was perhaps influenced by earlier unbuilt designs for exchanges by his fellow Frenchmen Tardieu and Bernard, whose designs of 1782 reveal the same monumental structure. Tardieu's design was based around a huge tunnel-vault and featured a similar arched window.

The severe Neo-Classicism of the French revolutionary period became a staple of bank, and particularly exchange, architecture. In fact for the first half of the nineteenth century it became *de rigeur* as an architectural suggestion of stability and financial dependability. Under Napoleon, the French gained confidence in the stability of the political system which had crumbled during the revolution and in 1800 the Banque de France was formed. Despite a series of designs for a national bank including a monumental design by Bergognon in 1790, in which he presaged the gigantic tunnel-vault of de Thomon's St Petersburg exchange, and the setting of a building for the national bank as

the Grand Prix of the French Academy in 1790, the bank when it was finally set up was squeezed into an existing building. The real architectural expression of growing French financial confidence was the Bourse, designed by Alexandre-Théodore Brongniart in 1808 and completed in 1826. This huge building, which was designed to provide a home for the Tribunal de Commerce as well as the stock exchange, remains one of Paris' best known landmarks. In style it shows the transition from Ledoux's monumentalism towards a softer Classicism, decorated with a frieze and employing slender Corinthian columns (as Vignon had begun to use at the Madeleine two years earlier). The Bourse building represents a move away from the Greek temple aesthetic which continued to dominate bank design elsewhere.

The same revolutionary ideals which had finally led France to found a national bank and to develop a new architectural language for its financial institutions also led to the breakaway from colonialism in North America. Perceiving the new republic to be the inheritor of the ideals of Athenian democracy, it was proper that Greek became the architectural language of choice for the newly independent America. The American economy was expanding rapidly, buoyed by expansion of the territory, abundant natural resources, improved transport, the introduction of machinery into agriculture and industry, and plentiful slave labour. The financial sector was booming by the beginning of the nineteenth century. Benjamin Henry Latrobe, who was born and began his career in England (although he had also attended school in Germany), started a new life in America in 1795 and one of his first significant buildings, the Bank of Pennsylvania in Philadelphia (1798-1800), was instrumental in adopting the temple front as the symbol of bank architecture. The Bank of Pennsylvania appears as a Roman temple, its domed circular banking hall providing the building's mass while the street frontage is formed by an Ionic portico raised on a plinth. That Latrobe was familiar with Soane's work is evident in the simplicity and clarity of his composition, in the elegance of the lantern and shallow dome which surmount the banking hall, and in the dramatic and sophisticated entry sequence which led from the vaulted vestibule, which began to suggest the form of the banking hall, to the expansive domed space beyond. But, despite Latrobe's success, it was one of the younger architects in his office who would define the Greek style as the architecture of American finance with an archaeological scheme for the Second National Bank of the United States, also in Philadelphia (1818-24). William Strickland, the bank's architect, won a competition with his design. The brief had already stipulated a Greek scheme to be executed in marble. Strickland merely took the brief to its extreme and created a copy of the Parthenon, fronting an impressive tunnel-vaulted banking hall, and thus instigated a period of archaeologically obsessive Greek revival in America. Strickland's other important work in the financial sphere was the Philadelphia Exchange (1832-34) in which he created an elegant solution for a difficult triangular site, a building which became a focal point and an important piece of urbanism. A number of both impressive and sometimes incompetent Greek revival banks were built in America over the next half century or so but few thereafter displayed the kind of skill or interest with which Latrobe and Strickland had initiated the style. The ensuing half century saw few major innovations in the field of bank architecture; buildings were largely dressed-up in historical fancy dress, even though the costumes often hid powerful spaces and impressive banking halls. The real advances in architectural form were confined to the burgeoning exchanges which underwent a resurgence not seen since the late Renaissance and which will be explored later.

THE DAWN OF THE MODERN ERA

In King Vidor's 1949 film of Ayn Rand's novel *The Fountainhead* we see a group of clients praising Howard Roark's (Gary Cooper) design for their new bank building. Pleased with the design they tell the architect (Roark) that they will build his scheme on condition that he agrees to some minor changes – at which point they begin to slot pieces of wedding-cake, Neo-Classical decoration on to Roark's powerfully stark, Miesian model. Roark refuses the conditions and the much needed commission – he will build only on his own terms – and goes off to work as a day labourer in a stone quarry. With a different ending, this episode would have proved an appropriate introduction to the dawn of modern financial architecture, although it comes from a film made about a century after the beginnings of the new architecture. For most of the nineteenth century and for the first half of the twentieth century (and arguably for the rest of it too),

the business of financial architecture was largely a question of the erection of a modern structure using newly available technologies and then the dressing of that structure up in appropriate clothing, just as the caricatured clients do in *The Fountainhead*.

The industrial revolution had brought about new engineering technologies which were quickly applied to architecture, chief among these were the advances made in building in iron. The engineers of the great railway stations were in the vanguard of the new building technology, but the engineering was largely separated from the architecture. The vast, cathedral-like roofs of the termini ran into brick and stone facades which were dressed up in all manner of historical styles. The facades were seen as architecture, the roofs as building. But it was to be the roofs of the great Victorian engineers that inspired the new architecture. The simplicity, clarity and transparency of these canopies led to a fundamental rethinking of architecture and, perhaps surprisingly, the patrons of the banks and exchanges were in the forefront of the movement to incorporate these new materials and structures.

The nineteenth century saw a critical change in patronage, the momentum transferred from the aristocracy and the nobility to the merchants, the bankers and the traders – the great magnates of the Victorian age. It was a change which mirrored in many ways the transferral of patronage in Renaissance Europe when the Church began to lose its position as key patron to the newly wealthy bankers and merchants, a change which occurred, as we have seen, with the most striking rapidity and impressive effects in fifteenth-century Florence. Like their Florentine forebears the new patrons wanted to flaunt their wealth, the buildings in which they traded and banked were to combine the best of the new technology with as much ornamentation as possible. The new generation of exchanges can be seen as approximations of the traditional type. Just as the Antwerp, Amsterdam and London exchanges of the sixteenth and seventeenth centuries were based around a large central courtyard, so the new exchanges of Europe revolved around a vast central space. But the technology in iron and glass now existed for that space to be covered and thus, as was the case with the stations, this building type encouraged the development of ever larger and more impressive glass canopies. The precursor of this new type of exchange was the Halle au Blè in Paris. The original building by

Lecamus de Mézières had been built between 1763 and 1768 and consisted of a circular plan based around a circular courtyard at its heart. The courtyard was enclosed by a timber dome designed by Legrand and Molinos in 1783 but was soon after destroyed in a fire. Its replacement was far more impressive – a glass dome with an iron structure designed by François-Joseph Bèlanger in 1808-13. The two most significant successors to Bèlanger's dome were both over the Channel in England. J B Bunning's London Coal Exchange (1846-49) has often been noted as a significant building in the development of Art Nouveau and consequently modern architecture (notably by Nikolaus Pevsner) and its use of an exposed iron structure, even if it is heavily ornamented, was a daring move by the architect. The building's Classical exterior gave way to a grand circular atrium overlooked by three tiers of iron galleries; this was the trading floor, light, airy and spacious, although the cantilevered iron galleries made it look somewhat like a prison interior. The same could be said of Cuthbert Brodrick's Corn Exchange in Leeds where an oval central space was covered by a similarly shaped dome. Brodrick's building, built between 1861-63, is an altogether more restrained and more elegant structure. A single gallery surrounds the space behind which windows give the effect of simple arcades. The building is less of a gasometer than Bunning's structure, although its roof is not as daring, only being partly glazed in the form of an elliptical oculus.

This type of building, the successor to the open courtyards of the early exchanges, using iron and glass to create the feel of a bright, open heart to the structure became an enduring model and to some extent survives today. The Third Royal Exchange in London (designed and built by Sir William Tite in 1838-44) was given a domed glass roof featuring unusual glazed pendentives in 1880, the Crèdit Lyonnais in Paris, designed by WOW Bouweins de Boijen, was given a huge and impressive glazed dome in 1908. This was perhaps inspired by the department stores which were springing up in Paris, most of which were designed around an elaborate atrium, but the form also owes something to Henri Labrouste's magnificent Bibliothèque Nationale of 1862-68. It was precisely this search for natural light and simplicity of structure which would lead to the banking hall of Otto Wagner's stripped Post Office Savings Bank (explored later). But there was another type of bank and exchange architec-

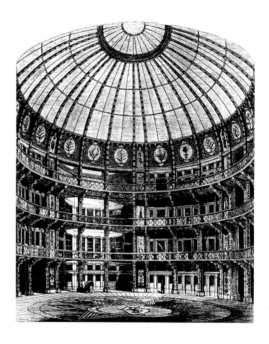

TOP: L de Mézières, Halle au Blé, 1763-68
CENTRE: JB Bunning, London Coal Exchange, 1846-49
BOTTOM: Lockwood and Mawson, Bradford Wood Exchange, 1864-67

TOP: Burnham and Root,
Chicago Insurance
Exchange, 1885
CENTRE: RN Shaw, Bradford
Exchange (Design), 1864
BOTTOM: Henry W Jones,
Bank of Commerce,
Minneapolis, 1888

ture which was developing at around the same time and which, when combined with the light atrium, would lead to H P Berlage's Amsterdam Exchange at the end of the nineteenth and beginning of the twentieth centuries. Berlage's exchange is also discussed later but its form is important to us at this point. Based on a type of National Romanticism blended with a structural functionalism, Berlage's building stands on the borders between Arts and Crafts, Historicism and Modernism. The building, with its huge brick tower, its asymmetry and galleried great hall, is based on a kind of archetypal Northern European or, more specifically, Flemish, medieval massing. The great bankers and the burghers of northern European cities began to look upon the medieval age as a golden era of trade, a period when northern Europe was able to formulate its own artistic styles and building types to suit the activities of its inhabitants, the climate and the local materials. When the Gothic style was chosen for the Houses of Parliament in London, designed by Sir Charles Barry and begun in 1835, it confirmed the style as a legitimate alternative to the then ubiquitous Classicism. Until then it would have been virtually inconceivable to design a bank, or an exchange, in anything other than the Classical style. Greek, Roman or Renaissance, each suggested a different type of strength, stability and taste, but each was accepted as a proper way of building. The introduction of Gothic to the financial world began in the middle of the nineteenth century and it was raised on the success of the monumental town halls of northern England. These were structures built by cities whose merchants revelled in their independence, their self-perceived image as paternalistic inheritors of a spurious Ruskinian vision of the past with their new-found wealth based on industry rather than class. Prominent British architects who worked with the Gothic vocabulary, principally George Gilbert Scott, argued for Gothic as the true and natural style for banks as it was synonymous with the medieval origins of modern Northern European banking. It had also come to represent the new wealth of the self-made middle classes as Classicism represented the landed establishment.

The new exchanges, which were set up to cater for the rapidly expanding northern European economies, first bore the Gothic style into the architecture of finance. Buoyed by the industrial revolution and exploding populations, German and British towns began to sprout exchanges with spiky towers and pointed arches. These were perceived by the men of business as the new market halls; prominent and impressive, they were very much the successors of the Flemish guild and cloth halls. The first use of Gothic was the Frankfurt Exchange designed by F August Stüler in 1839, the interior of which was based around a curious fan-vaulted hall, although the building remained resolutely Classical from the outside. Heinrich Müller's Bremen Exchange (1861-64) was more convincingly Gothic with a great ecclesiastical nave, while the Bradford Wool Exchange by Lockwood and Mawson (1864-67) is a fine example of Victorian civic Gothic, complete with clock tower (time is money after all). One of the other entrants in the competition to design the Bradford Exchange was that by the young Richard Norman Shaw. His design, a romantic and solid medieval scheme with a monumental belfry-like tower, brought with it the seeds of an architectural approach which would come to maturity in Berlage's Amsterdam exchange over three decades later. Although Shaw's design was picturesque and 'changeful' (to use the Ruskinian word), in its massing and medieval simplicity, this was an important design which encapsulated the beginning of an Arts and Crafts architecture. The obsession with the picturesque meant that the British Arts and Crafts or Freestyle rarely transferred to the city comfortably or successfully and remained a largely rural and, ultimately, suburban adventure. Berlage and his German contemporaries would remodel this mix of national Romanticism and Ruskinian honesty into a more potent blend of the seemingly oxymoronic functional picturesque which subsequently laid the roots of Modernism.

While the medieval cloth hall was becoming an acceptable role model for the architecture of exchanges, the Renaissance *palazzo* remained entrenched as its principal inspiration. Wimmel and Forsmann's Hamburg Exchange (1837-41), Theophil von Hansen's Vienna Exchange (1869-77) and Burnitz and Sommer's Frankfurt Exchange (1874-79), the building which succeeded Stüler's fan-vaulted perpendicular exercise of 1839, all took the grand palace as their model and many came to resemble the great opera houses, such as Garnier's Opera in Paris, which were then being built. In some designs the influence of the pared-down industrial warehouse can be seen being combined with the *palazzo* aesthetic to create a

new, monumental type based on the repetition of (often Byzantine or Venetian) detail. George B Post's New York Produce Exchange (1881-85)and Union Trust Building (1889) are perhaps the clearest examples of this new blend while Burnham and Root's Chicago Insurance Exchange (completed the same year)and Harry Wild Jones' Bank of Commerce, Minneapolis (1888) exhibit the same kind of industrial Byzantine.

Meanwhile changes in the architecture of banks were less dramatic but nevertheless significant. The Gothic style never really came to compete with the Classical in bank architecture as it had done in the exchanges: Renaissance and Neo-Classical remained the prescribed styles. From 1826, legislation was passed which allowed the formation of Joint Stock banks in England, although the Bank of England retained the right to print money. This led to a building type new to England, the branch bank, a building which soon became a staple component of main streets throughout England and indeed Europe. At the beginning of the evolution of this new building type, the building was still split between commercial and residential functions. The boss, and sometimes his staff and clerks too, still lived over the shop and consequently the branch bank was in many ways the direct successor to the great Florentine palaces of the Renaissance banking dynasties. What had of course changed was that a public space was introduced into the heart of the bank, the banking hall; the building was to be open and inviting to the public yet at the same time closed and secure to the robber. Security was a key functional and aesthetic theme, as it had been for the builders of the Renaissance palaces. All over Europe riots and revolutions were commonplace throughout the nineteenth century; the banks had to be secure not only against robbers but against mobs and revolutionaries and against fire. The bank became a fortress, defended with guns which were almost invariably kept on the premises, and at its heart was the huge, impenetrable safe. The building had to pivot around the explicitly public banking hall and the privacy and security of the safe.

As a result of the desire for physical and visual security these new branch banks did not imitate the architectural expression of the shops which surrounded them, although increasingly they were offering a range of services and had become more than ever a form of money shop. Instead they were created as a reinterpretation of the traditional image of the bank as a grand palace. The Classical architectonic language remained the *lingua franca* of bank architects and a series of innovative architectural treatments was devised to accommodate the functions of the bank. CR Cockerell's Liverpool Branch of the Bank of England (1844-47) eloquently displays the contortions of Classical form which were employed to provide a banking hall, offices and dwelling space, while other branches at Bristol and Manchester show him refining a style which ingeniously stretched the Classical vocabulary to accommodate the needs of the modern bank. John Gibson's National Provincial Bank of England (now the NatWest Bank) in Bishopsgate, London (1865) showed a similar approach to Soane's nearby Bank of England, the building portrayed as a single-storey mass behind a great screen wall. Like the Bank of England this was a multi-storey structure but cunningly disguised: property prices were too expensive to allow the building of a single storey on such a prestigious site. In fact it was precisely the realisation that there was profit to be made in building extra, rentable office space into a new bank building which paved the way for the proto-skyscrapers in American cities that presaged the advent of the blend of bank and speculative office characteristic of much twentieth-century bank design.

Although the Neo-Classical remained the dominant architectural language for banks throughout the nineteenth century, other styles played a role, albeit a lesser one. The Baroque palace was the inspiration for the great banks of Central Europe. J F Wanner's Schweizerische Kreditanstalt in Zurich (1873), Friedrich von Schmidt's Bayerische Hypotheken-und-Wechselbank in Munich (1895-98) were *tours-de-force* of a kind of urban Baroque which sprang from Haussmann's Paris boulevards and Vienna's Ringstrasse. The medieval and the Gothic made appearances in Norman Shaw's mock Tudor Capital and Counties Bank, Farnham (1868), G M Tilley's Lloyds Bank, Glastonbury (1885), Leopold Eidlitz's Dry Dock Savings Bank, New York (1875), the latter executed in a kind of Waterhouse Victorian mansion style and Frank Furness' wonderfully weird National Bank of the Republic, Philadelphia (1883-84), wedged into a tight urban site with a fairy-tale Gothic stair-turret rising through its centre.

The only other style which could compete with Neo-Classical, Renaissance and Gothic was the Byzantine which began to be favoured by a number of American banks. America was the fertile ground from which these Byzantine structures appeared and their undisputed master was Louis Sullivan. Although the great rounded arches and cavernous spaces which appeared in these new banks were stylistically reminiscent of the Byzantine revival, they proved to be among the first buildings which looked substantially beyond matters of style since Soane's Bank of England. Just as Berlage's Amsterdam Exchange hid its modernity behind an impression of medieval solidity, so the blocky masses of the new American banks bore within them the seeds of great advances in design. Sullivan and George B Post, mentioned earlier, both contributed greatly to the development of the skyscraper. By the time he built the National Farmers' Bank in Owatonna, Minnesota (1906-08) Sullivan had already undergone a severe decline in popularity and in the number of commissions he was awarded. The designs of his masterpieces the Chicago Auditorium Building (1886-90), the Wainwright Building (1890) and the Guaranty Building (1894-95) were over a decade behind him and despite his pivotal role in developing a language of modern urban architecture he had fallen out of favour. Becoming embittered at a world which seemed to refuse to recognise his genius, his decline and descent into alcoholism and depression were arrested in part by a string of bank buildings completed in the first two decades of the twentieth century. Some of his monumental earlier buildings and projects housed or envisaged potential banking functions, notably the Guaranty Building and the remarkable unbuilt 1893 design for the St. Louis Trust and Savings Building. But it was only with these bank buildings in the Mid West, which were his last significant commissions, that he began to work decisively and influentially in the banking oeuvre. His buildings eloquently expressed the massive dignity and solidity of the huge central banking halls (huge in relation to the size of these tiny agricultural communities) with a kind of Roman monumentality. They appeared on the landscape of American architecture as an almost lone voice against the dominant Beaux Arts Classicism. Frank Lloyd Wright had also worked on designs for banks (which, in a curious role reversal, may in turn have influenced his master, Sullivan) and Purcell, Feick and Elmslie designed a very successful bank in the Sullivan manner with the Merchants Bank of Winona in 1911-12.

The Beaux Arts style had exerted an unbreakable influence on American architecture in the wake of its successes at the Chicago Worlds Fair of 1893. Its best known and most robust practitioners, who had themselves contributed significantly to the architecture of the Worlds Fair, were undoubtedly McKim, Mead and White. One of their earliest large commissions, the American Safe Deposit Company and Columbia Bank Building in New York (1882-84), was an essay in the translation of the language of the Italian *palazzo* into a multi-storey structure (in this case eight storeys). In the midst of a depression the practice managed to build the grand and theatrical Neo-Classical Bowery Savings Bank in New York (1893-95) and a few years later the more subdued, freestanding, State Savings Bank in Detroit, Michigan (1898-1900). McKim, Mead and White greeted the new century with a series of other impressive banks, the enlargement of the existing Bank of Montreal in Montreal (1903-05), the wonderful Knickerbocker Trust Building in New York (1901-04), where the architects skilfully used a giant Corinthian order to house all the building's four floors, and the National City Bank in the same city, where a taller building is split into two levels of colonnades enclosing a highly impressive top-lit banking room. Their unexecuted design for the National City Bank, New York, of 1909, however, revealed the weaknesses of their approach when compared to Sullivan's easy mastery of the tall building form, proposing a simple superimposition of a skyscraper on to a Beaux Arts base with a domed banking hall.

Beaux Arts remained the dominant style for banks in North America just as Neo-Georgian and Neo-Classical became *de rigeur* for English banks, while Baroque and Renaissance dominated continental European bank and exchange architecture. At the turn of the century a handful of buildings was responsible for changing the conception of bank architecture and although the First World War and the conservatism which ensued created an obstacle to a continuous line of development, it is to these buildings that we can trace the genesis of the bank architecture of Modernism which by and large has survived and become the dominant force in the architecture of international finance. The buildings to which I refer include a trio of fascinating departures from the contemporary norm: these are Berlage's Amsterdam Stock Exchange, Otto Wagner's Post Office Savings Bank in Vienna (1904-06) and Ödön Lechner's Post Office Savings Bank in Budapest (1899-1902). The other group of buildings that prompts a re-examination of the principles of bank design is the portfolio of Louis H Sullivan. The changes defined by this disparate group of buildings are so important and played (and to some extent continue to play) such a pivotal role in the formulation of a new language of bank architecture that it is necessary to look at the achievements of the architects in a series of separate chapters before we can look at further developments in the ensuing century.

George B Post, Union Trust Building, New York City, 1889-90

HP Berlage, Amsterdam Exchange, 1898-1903; TOP: West elevation; BOTTOM: Interior, Produce Exchange

THE AMSTERDAM STOCK EXCHANGE
H P Berlage

Amsterdam had risen to prominence as the capital of European trade in the seventeenth century; it overtook the Italian cities in importance and was subsequently overtaken itself by the ascendence of London as the pre-eminent centre for European trade. When H P Berlage was commissioned to design a huge new stock exchange for the city in 1896 it was therefore logical to look to the Dutch Renaissance for inspiration. It is interesting, in the light of London's eclipsing of Amsterdam's pre-eminence, that Berlage's most important influence, beside the architecture of the Dutch Renaissance period, should have been the British legacy of Ruskin and Morris; the search for an honest, national building style. The Dutch, at the end of the nineteenth century, were profoundly aware of the decline of their country's status as a world power. Berlage's building was to be not only an important centre of finance and exchange but also a symbol of the resurrection of the country's fortunes; a statement of a rediscovered pride and confidence, very much as the great exchanges of the mid-nineteenth century had been in Britain. The developments in British architecture had been a reaction to the industrial revolution, some exploiting new techniques and structures which had been developed through advances in technology, others a conservative reaction to what was seen as the impersonal horror of mass production. In Holland the industrial revolution had come considerably later than in the country's northern European neighbours and in a curious way Berlage's building embodies both a mature appreciation of the benefits of technology and a cautious Historicism which draws on, but does not ape, the styles of the past; an approach more akin to the socialist architects of the Arts and Crafts Movement, such as W R Lethaby who recognised the importance of accepting and using new materials and technologies.

The design occupies the whole of a massive, irregular site at the centre of commercial Amsterdam. Berlage abhorred the masking of materials with cladding or render and, as a result, the Exchange stands as a huge mountain of exposed (honest) brick. Although based on the language of sixteenth- and seventeenth-century Dutch architecture, there are also significant overtones of Byzantine mass in the arches and the huge, undecorated surfaces which impress through their scale rather than their decoration. At the same time the building is strongly reminiscent of the town halls of the Italian Renaissance with its arcades and campanile – Venice and Siena both come to mind. The idea behind this is obviously that such a building should represent the city itself, a city built on trade and exchange, just as it was the wealth springing from trade and financial dealings of those Italian cities which enabled them to erect such monumental edifices.

Berlage took some time to reach his conclusion about the final appearance of the Exchange; it was after all a monumental task as the building was not only to be massive but was to present a version of the city's self image, it was to be a structure which would define the new vision of the city. The design went through a series of radical changes from the first version which was presented in a blend of the Romanesque, the Byzantine monumentality of H H Richardson and perhaps a hint of Alfred Waterhouse's robust High Victorianism. The building encompassed a multitude of spaces and functions appropriate to its status as a new civic centre. Three great halls formed its core and these were devoted to commodities, corn and stock exchange. Along with these came the associated offices for brokers and a new chamber of commerce; other functions within the building included a restaurant, post office and telephone exchange and a strong-room below the structure. The halls accommodating the exchanges were required to

create an imposing and impressive effect as they were also to house great civic functions, official ceremonies and meetings.

The huge hall of the commodities exchange is very much the heart of the building, the other spaces feed off it and, to some extent, are merely variations on the same theme. The lofty space is overlooked by arcaded galleries and lit by a glazed roof which itself is supported on a series of brightly painted, delicate iron trusses. The monumental, heavy effect which defines the exterior is absent here and the building appears light, bright and airy; a fascinating blend of the medieval and the High Tech in a manner reminiscent of Deane and Woodward's Oxford Museum (1855-60) or the great Victorian railway stations. It has often been noted that the play of planes in this space, particularly in the intersection of the buttresses supporting the trusses and the arcades and in the cleanly expressed junctions which occur throughout, were precursors of the approach which led to the innovations of the De Stijl Movement, where buildings are reduced to a series of pure planes and it is the pattern of intersections which creates space. At the same time there is also great depth, a harsh northern light and a simplicity of space which recalls the work of the great Dutch painters of the seventeenth century from Vermeer to De Hooch and the carefully controlled, austere yet human interior worlds which they created. Just as those seventeenth-century painters had given their works a solid base of proportional control and imposed upon them rigorous grids and structuring devices, so Berlage's building is based on a meticulous proportional system which had enthralled Dutch architects of the *fin-de-siècle* period.

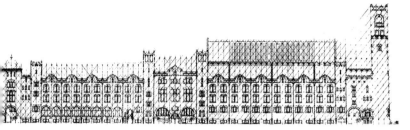

Elevation showing proportional system

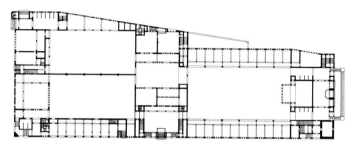

Plan

Each space is based on a given number of squares within the grid. The grid itself is based on the proportions of a pyramid which Viollet-le-Duc had described and which became known as the 'Egyptian triangle' (although it was derived from studies of Gothic architecture). The proportional system governs the building in three dimensions; the elevations (windows, gables, towers and roofs) as well as the elements of the plan are controlled by the base to height ratio of 8:5.

Although the Amsterdam Exchange is a rather severe building which imposes itself on the city through its mass and the expansive brick surfaces which it exposes, it is not lacking in decoration. To maintain the power and the visual effect of unbroken vertical planes, Berlage recessed all the decoration into the depth of the walls. In doing this he was emphasising the bulk of the structure by revealing its massive depth as well as maintaining the integrity of the planes, which is what Soane had done at the Bank of England a century earlier. It also meant that the decorative elements appeared more fully integrated into the structure of the building, inherent rather than applied, and in this the architect was fulfilling the Arts and Crafts ideal of the building as *Gesamtkunstwerk*. In fact some of the foremost Dutch artists of the period were involved in the building's decoration including Jan Toorop, one of the key figures in the development of Art Nouveau, Lambertus Zijl and Mendes da Costa who executed a series of sculptures and reliefs around the building. Berlage himself designed the furniture and the exquisite understated detailing which characterises the building.

Among the plethora of important financial buildings which sprang up around the turn of the century, Berlage's building perhaps best embodies the paradoxes of the period. Both backward and forward-looking it is a pure example of the Arts and Crafts ideal which, although it has been often cited as a forerunner of modern architecture, is very much of, rather than ahead of, its time. Yet it is a supremely functional building, its contents are clearly expressed on the elevations, its rational plan produces a rational building; everything is done for a reason. But it remains far from functionalism: Berlage himself was present at the first CIAM meeting in 1928 and followed the emergence of the Modern Movement with interest, but despite his status as one of its pioneers he remained sceptical (as did his English counterpart Lethaby) of the emerging architectonic language of functionalism. Ultimately the significance of the Amsterdam Exchange is twofold. Firstly, it represents a frank recognition of the importance of trade to the existence of the city; it is a building synonymous with the wealth which founded the city and consequently with the city itself. Secondly, it acts as a bridge between the nineteenth and twentieth centuries; just as its building spanned the juncture between the two centuries so it remains a symbol of the often paradoxical position of the turn-of-the-century architects who were as impressed by the new technology and the notion of a functional plan as the generator of a building's form as they were by the Gothic cathedral and the Renaissance Italian city. If there is a cathedral to money in Europe, a building which attempts to sculpt the city around itself and to appear a bastion of permanence in a sea of financial volatility, then Berlage's Amsterdam Stock Exchange is that building.

POST OFFICE SAVINGS BANK, VIENNA
OTTO WAGNER

If there is one bank building which embodies the change from a nineteenth- to a twentieth-century architecture it is undoubtedly Wagner's Imperial and Royal Post Office Savings Bank in Vienna (1904-06). Curiously there is very little that is revolutionary in style in Wagner's bank, in fact it represents the continuation of a line of traditional bank buildings within which most of the organisational features and other motifs are still clearly recognisable. The building is based on the established pattern of organisation around a central hall which is lit from above and surrounded by the desks of the tellers. It follows essentially the same plan as the early exchanges and money markets with buildings surrounding courtyards, except that affairs here are carried out under a glazed roof rather than the open sky. The central space itself can be compared to the traditional basilica section with a tall central nave and side aisles which house the counters.

Wagner had considerable experience designing buildings for finance; his competition design in 1880 for the central offices of the Vienna Giro- und Kassenverein (Deposit and Current Account Banking Association) was placed third. It was a clear, rational treatment of an awkward site, far superior to the jumbled and wasteful plan of the victors. A circular lobby led to a grand processional route culminating in a semi-circular bank of tellers' desks and offices arranged in an apsidal form. So successful and logical was this plan that Wagner adopted it for his design for the Länderbank in Vienna (1882-84). Again the architect used a circular lobby, in this instance to address an awkward site and effect a sudden change in axis. In turn, this arrangement of a top-lit central banking space would inform Wagner's later design for the Post Office Savings Bank. Wagner's competition design for the offices of the Austrian Bodenkreditanstalt (1884) was the other important experiment in the develop-

ment of the ideas he would later use in the Post Office Savings Bank. In this design the lobby is based around a grand staircase which gives access to a rectangular banking hall surrounded by offices in an arrangement very similar to the one he would later employ. In the same year he also submitted a grandiose and altogether inappropriate design for the Amsterdam Exchange in which Berlage was successful. His design, a huge Baroque wedding cake, is a good indicator of just how successful Berlage's design was.

The designs for the Post Office Savings Bank however date from almost two decades later. By this time Wagner had perfected his ideas about a Modern Architecture which he outlined in the book of that name and first published in 1895. His rational approach can be compared in many ways with that of Louis H Sullivan: the notion of form following function was used as a mantra by both architects. Like Sullivan, Wagner was a key figure in the international phenomenon which can be loosely defined as Art Nouveau, in fact, he was instrumental in the formation and continuing success of the Viennese Secession, even if his own work was often more rational and Classical than that of his Art Nouveau peers. Whereas Sullivan remained attached to his organic mode of decoration throughout the series of banks he designed in the first decades of the twentieth century, the Post Office Savings Bank defines a critical moment in the career of Wagner where he perhaps first effectively realised his goal of a functional, modern architecture. Sullivan's banks are a wonderful post-script to a career which culminated in his ideas about skyscrapers and his executed tall buildings. His banks were masterpieces of symbolism and design, which were resurrected from obscurity by historians keen to point out the pluralist roots of early modern architecture as a way of justifying the departures from Functionalist orthodoxy which led to Post-Modernism. However it was Wagner's building which was to be the great influence on the development of Modernism itself, even though it was completed two years before the building of Sullivan's Owatonna Farmers' Bank.

Some background is necessary to understand the period and the functions, both physical and symbolic, which were crystallised so effectively by Wagner in the Post Office Savings Bank and to explore why the building had such a powerful and lasting effect on the development of modern architecture. The Imperial Postal Savings Bank was founded in the 1880s by civil servant Georg Coch to give the average person the chance to open a bank account even with a small amount of money. The institution was meant as a force to counterbalance the immense wealth and power of the great private banks. By encouraging thousands of individuals to begin saving (it was possible to make deposits and withdrawals at the existing network of post offices without having to go to a purpose-built bank) the Postal Savings Bank soon grew into a formidable institution with a democratic remit, to protect and supplement the small savings of the working and lower middle classes. Admirable and egalitarian as this may seem, there was a sinister political motive behind the move, that of anti-semitism. Anti-semitism was rife in Central Europe during this period and it was fuelled by envy; the Jews had become extremely powerful in the field of banking and the great banking clans dominated the European financial markets. The Rothschilds were perhaps the best known and indeed the powerful Jewish liberal tendency was referred to as the 'Rothschild Party'. Georg Coch, the Savings Bank's founder, became an icon of the anti-semites and although his supporters failed to have his bust displayed inside the bank's new headquarters due to opposition from Jewish groups, Karl Lueger, Vienna's

Cutaway drawing of Post Office Savings Bank, Vienna

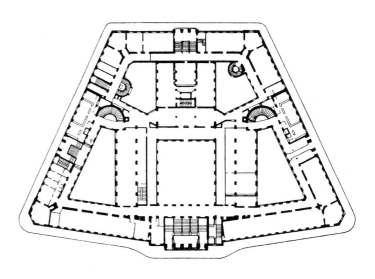

Post Office Savings Bank, Vienna

ardently anti-semitic Christian Socialist mayor, led a successful campaign to install Coch's bust in the square outside the building where it still stands as a reminder of the bank's questionable founding ideals.

The architectural context of the bank can be said to have been made by Wagner himself who was almost solely responsible for the development of the purpose-built business and office block. This departed from the model which had become the Viennese and Central European standard of the mixed-use block combining retail, office and residential accommodation within a single building. His Länderbank of 1882 displays a stripped, self-effacing facade to the street concealing a huge bank building, an elevation which eschews the Baroque moulding and detail which characterises so much of late nineteenth-century Viennese architecture. The elevations to the interior courtyards and light wells reveal the stripped Functionalism which the architect was working towards but was not yet able to express in such a conservative age. Here, at the back end of the building, simple blocky piers rise through the storeys and are expressed on the outside of the structure while the windows are brought flush with the completely unadorned, rendered facade. The elevation is treated as a skin through which holes are punched; the purpose of which is simply to let natural light into the offices which surround the central banking hall. These spaces would otherwise have been small and unlit. Wagner's plan addresses this problem with flair and imagination, the internal hierarchy of the building is broken down and lowly clerks are given spacious and well-lit offices just as those higher up the banking hierarchy are accommodated in clean, bright rooms. The public is treated to a grand display of democratic space, clear delineation of function and bountiful natural light from above.

The same preoccupations defined Wagner's approach to the Postal Savings Bank. Despite the vast scale of the building its appearance and its public entrance are understated and unassuming; there is no deliberate show of wealth or ostentation here as that would be seen as running against the 'democratic' ideals upon which the bank was founded. As such the building does not attempt to draw attention to itself through grandiosity or monumentality despite the fact that it is a gigantic complex opening on to a public square just off the Ringstrasse. It is interesting to note that in Wagner's composite drawing submitted to the

original design competition in 1903, the building appears in a perspective while crowds of people melt into the site plan which occupies the lower half of the drawing. It is as if the city, the people and the new building were one. This is precisely the effect that Wagner was after, a truly public building which would become part of the machinery of the rational, functioning, modern city. The building's facade also had to embody the principles of the bank's foundation and, consequently, it is the main elevation which presents perhaps the most interesting exposition of Wagner's architectural philosophy. Vienna's Ringstrasse architecture, to which Wagner himself had significantly contributed, was defined by a Neo-Renaissance style in which the detail and effect were provided by plaster mouldings and decorative render; each building resembling a mini Florentine palace. In developing his theories on a 'Modern Architecture' Wagner began to abhor the idea of cladding the wall with a material which imitated any other material, usually stone. He also disliked the deep modelling of the elevation which he regarded as archaic and unsuited to the polluted urban environment as it was hard to maintain and keep clean. His inspiration was Gustav Klimt whose pictorial work introduced a new vision of what could be done in the two-dimensional plane of the picture. His language of decoration based on a flat surface, suggesting a depth which was other than physical, deeply moved Wagner. This corresponded in many ways with Gottfried Semper's highly influential ideas about the wall as the inheritor of the legacy of the protective fabric of the tent which he saw as the archetypal vertical building surface. The facade of the Postal Savings Bank is protected by a coating of granite and marble slabs. This cladding performs a series of visual and symbolic functions: the individual panels help to break up the huge mass of the walls; the granite panels serve to differentiate the lower (public) floors of the building from the upper office storeys; the bolts which help to fix the panels to the walls are covered by aluminium caps. These create a decorative effect throughout the elevation but also make clear the fact that these blocks are cladding, rather than structural. In fact these aluminium caps are deliberately reminiscent of the rivets in the hull of a ship or in the body of a steam-engine – they are a symbolic reminder of the rational function of the bank as a money machine. At the same time the preciseness of the cladding panels, the relative

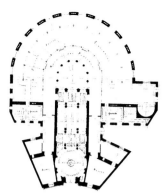

Giro und Kassenverein, Wagner's design, 1880, ground plan

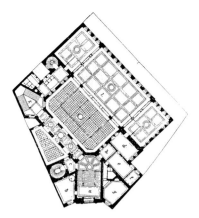

Emil von Foster's winning design, 1880, ground plan

luxury of the materials and the silver studs in each corner of the panels combine to give a feeling of preciousness. It is as if what was contained inside the building deserves this special protective coat. At once, Wagner achieves an effect of physical lightness, of consistent visual interest, of luxury without opulence and manages to maintain the symbolic function of heavy rustication both binding the building into its urban context and creating a heavy plinth to elevate the building and articulate the preciousness of its contents. The architect's cutaway perspective of the facade reveals a paper-thin wall, a diaphanous screen which separates the public from the private realm yet does not suggest that either realm is more important. Inside and out, public and private, bank and square – it is a continuity of democratic urban space.

A similar paradox is embodied in the unassuming glass canopy which surmounts the building's main public entrance. The riveted steel elements and the glass canopy are borrowed from marine architecture, an architecture which has shed tradition in the interest of economy and function. It is a mark of the bank's frugality and openness that there seems to be nothing wasteful in the architecture, the bank must not be seen to be squandering the common man's money on luxurious offices for the managers. The sleekness, clarity and economy of naval architecture are continued within the building. The cool, light marble cladding which defines the interior of the lobby and takes the visitor up the steps to the main banking hall is unfussy and clean; steel heating grilles and balusters maintain the image of an efficient machine. The banking hall itself is a revelation. The space is expansive and open, more like a railway station concourse than a bank and it is precisely this openness and the deliberate lack of exclusivity and pomposity which makes this such a self-consciously democratic space. This room is the precursor of the Modernist glass house where all is transparency and light, the darkness and impenetrability of

shadowed corners and unseen nooks are banished to the world of the previous century. The great glass roof is visibly merely a skin, it seems to have no weight and its lack of structural significance is emphasised by the steel columns which pierce it and which can be seen continuing in vague outline through the milky glass of the panes. The structure meets the floor at the tiniest of points, the junctions are confined to riveted slender steel columns which define the central nave of the basilica form. The floor is also of glass; panels of glass blocks allow natural light into the lower floors in an improvement of the system Wagner first tried out at the Länderbank. As on the elevations, decoration exists only very subtly, a far cry from the contemporary excesses of the Secessionists. Visual interest is given by the detailing: rivets on the steel members, functional, utilitarian lamps hanging from the columns, geometric steel reliefs and decorative inlay are barely visible yet help to give a feeling of clarity and the impression that every form, every surface and every element fulfils a function and a need, that there is nothing superfluous. If anything is celebrated within the building it is the services. The utilitarian electric lights hang like ripe fruit from the slender steel columns, the piers between the doors and counters are celebrated by the shiny aluminium heating columns which again hint at the marine inspiration of the building's forms. The heating in fact was highly sophisticated. As well as the hot-air piping system which heated the building through the aluminium blowers mentioned above, there was an additional heating system beneath the roof to keep it free from snow. The sophisticated tensile structure supporting the glass roof presaged the developments of a self-consciously High-Tech architecture in the second half of the twentieth century, and also anticipated its failures. The heating system, for instance, was necessarily sophisticated and powerful to counterbalance the building's hopeless insulation and the amount of heat lost through the huge expanse of glass.

Competition design for Amsterdam Exchange, 1884

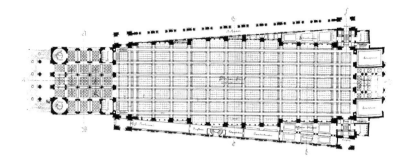

The almost endless rows of offices were separated by moveable partitions, a considerable innovation at the time. Only the board rooms and governors' offices feature more traditional timber panelling and these too are austere and functional spaces; the panelling echoes the forms which can be seen on the columns in the banking hall.

In the light of this rigorous utilitarianism and a denial of other than purely geometric decoration, it is perhaps surprising to see the main elevation crowned by a pair of angels. On early drawings (from around 1903) a pair of figural sculptural groups was proposed. These were based around the figure of Mercury or Hermes, the messenger of the gods. He is recognisable by the wings on his heels and the *caduceus* (the staff with a pair of serpents coiled around it which has become the symbol of medicine) he carries, although unusually he also holds a laurel wreath and has wings on his back. Mercury, associated with swiftness and guile, became the symbol of both bankers and thieves. He was also associated with alchemy, the attempt to create gold from base metal (hence also the medical use of the god as a symbol for the curative powers of the profession), the creation of value from nothing – or interest as it is now known. As the building's ornamentation was reduced in subsequent designs these sculptural groups were replaced by a pair of single figures, female angels whose wings were formed by the sides of great curved upstands tying them back to the parapet. Each angel holds a pair of laurel wreaths and the wreath motif appears again behind the figures on a recessed attic-storey screen wall and at the sides of the parapet. Although they are stiff and Classical, far less flowing than the original Secessionist designs, they terminate the building in a striking manner. They remind me of the angels looking down on the city in Wim Wenders' film *The Wings of Desire*, beings from another realm reaching out to the physical realm which is embodied by the rationalism of Wagner's great building.

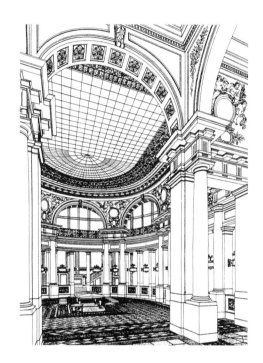

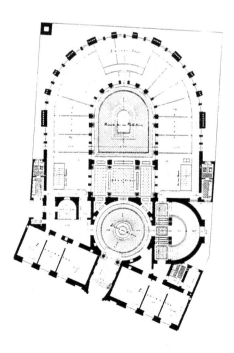

TOP: Amsterdam Exchange, design
CENTRE: Länderbank, interior
BOTTOM: Länderbank, plan

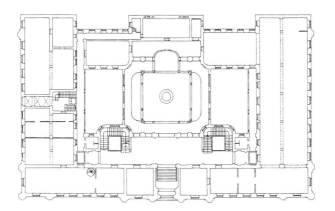

Postal Savings Bank, Budapest

POSTAL SAVINGS BANK, BUDAPEST
Ödön Lechner

Although this essay follows that on Wagner's Postal Savings Bank in Vienna, to have been chronologically accurate, it should have preceded any discussion about Wagner's building, as Ödön Lechner's building was completed three years before Wagner's was begun. It is perhaps significant that the two architects, respectively the most important architects in their countries at this time, were friends. Wagner's bank is unquestionably the more important of the two in the history of international twentieth-century architecture; it has exerted a powerful influence on the development of modern design and is one of the most iconic and recognisable of the buildings claimed as the precursors of twentieth-century Modernism. Lechner's building is less well known because it does not stand as part of a perceptible direct line of development within the Modern movement, rather, it seems to stand on its own as a remarkable but wonderful freak. Yet this is not entirely the case; in many ways it both fits into the development of modern architecture and confounds the expectations and norms of the era to stand as one of the most fascinating and rich bank buildings, easily bearing comparison with Wagner's masterpiece.

The background to the Postal Savings Bank as an institution in Hungary is broadly similar to that in Vienna. It was set up as a bank to encourage ordinary citizens to save, it was to be the bank of the people, their savings would be guaranteed by the state. In Budapest, as in its sister capital of the Austro-Hungarian Empire, Vienna, the foundation of the Postal Savings Bank was seen as a force to counterbalance the enormous wealth and power of the private banks. Some of the same anti-semitic sentiments were responsible for this attempt to break what was perceived as a Jewish stranglehold on the economy. But in Budapest there was an extra dimension, that of Hungarian nationalism. Since 1867, Hungary had been given an

unprecedented degree of autonomy within the empire. Budapest was outstripped only by Chicago in its growth and development as a major industrial city at the turn of the century, both industry and agriculture were thriving and Hungary's capital was proud and keen to show its wealth to the world and to compete with Vienna which was looking increasingly conservative and dowdy. The bulk of the city's architecture followed the same pattern as Vienna; mixed-use urban blocks accommodating retail, commercial and residential premises based on vaguely Neo-Renaissance and Baroque architectural types. Lechner was in the vanguard of the few architects who were looking to express the Hungarian-ness in architecture and who attempted to resist the pervasive influence of the Viennese model. They were keen that Budapest should not become a second-rate version of the capital of the empire, but rather a capital city in its own right with an architecture to express the past, present and future of its people.

Lechner, however, rejected Historicism or Eclecticism, in fact, he was one of the first major European architects to find real alternatives to the accepted catalogue of styles and types for large-scale urban public buildings. He had been in England and was impressed with the work of the Arts and Crafts architects, although he himself was less reliant on the vernacular as a source. What had impressed him more, however, was the work of British architects who designed buildings in the colonies. He was fascinated by how the British architects used motifs and symbolism from native cultures and incorporated them into what remained recognisably and resolutely British imperial buildings. He questioned how it was that Hungarian architects could not even manage to define or articulate a language which was Hungarian, let alone create such a robust architectural language that it could stand combining with other styles and elements yet retain its essential integrity.

Lechner made this search for a Hungarian mode of expression his life's work and in a series of exceptional and eccentric buildings he began to create what he saw as a genuinely Hungarian architecture. What was unusual about his work was that it stood apart from both the Art Nouveau and Secessionist Movements and from National Romanticism which was just at this time emerging as a force in European architecture. He shared the ideal of the National Romantics, the desire to create a recognisable language which combines nostalgia for a lost age and hope that those past glories can be recaptured through art and revolution in the new century. However, he was in many ways as rational an architect as his contemporary Wagner and he was not interested in reviving a language of architectonic elements in order to create yet another new style, as National Romantic architects had done throughout Europe. Instead he became engrossed in the work of ethnographers and cultural historians who had begun to trace the history of the Hungarian people to their roots in Central Asia. Through the examination of contemporary research and writing about symbols and motifs in folk art, embroidery and costume and through artefacts and archaeology Lechner began to formulate a language of symbols and forms which he regarded as coming from the well of the Hungarian nation, pure and unadulterated by nostalgia or whimsy. His work can helpfully be compared to that of the Hungarian composers Bartók and Kodály who followed him in researching the roots of Hungarian art (or in their case music) and used these archaic systems and languages to create new forms of art. Bartók and Kodály were among the foremost innovators in modern music. By combining modern ideas and harmonies with the ancient tonal systems and curious melodies of Hungarian folk music they took modern music to a new plane. It was as if the soul of the people added the necessary ingredient which gave music that might otherwise have been too abstract or difficult a grounding in some kind of Jungian unconscious, making it both appealing and dramatic and enabling it to touch a deep well-spring of emotional response.

Lechner attempted to do just that in architecture. Rather than reviving architectures from the past, Lechner strove to forge a new way of building using rational planning, modern, innovative structural tech-

nologies and materials. He then employed motifs and symbolism derived from what he saw as ancient Hungarian archetypes in order to give the rational building a soul and to root it in Hungarian culture. Lechner designed a series of important public buildings each of which was critical in the new definition of the Hungarian nation. These included the Museum of Applied Arts (1891-96), which was the first major European museum to be designed in a non-historicist style, and the Institute of Geology (1898-99), both in Budapest. The Postal Savings Bank was to be his third and last major public building, after its completion a new age of reaction set in and Lechner's architecture fell out of favour.

The building represents an unusual blend of structural rationalism and a rich and fantastical reservoir of decorative symbolic elements. The building is also highly unusual in that it manages to retain a great simplicity while indulging in this rich iconographic and decorative programme. The elevations create a striking contrast with the heavily sculpted Neo-Renaissance buildings which make up its context. The heavy rustication, deeply shadowed mouldings and decorative sculptures which adorn the surrounding buildings are completely absent here. Like Wagner, Lechner treated the facade like a textile in a manner obviously inspired by the writings of Gottfried Semper who saw the wall as a derivative of the fabric of a tent and the woven tapestry which was hung upon the vertical surface. Otto Wagner, Max Fabiani and Adolf Loos evolved similar elevational treatments in their Viennese buildings at around the same time. But whereas each of these architects punched geometric openings into a flat facade which was generally tiled with a Secessionist or more abstract geometric pattern, Lechner was keen to emphasise the textile metaphor and consequently used decorative motifs and colours from Hungarian folk art and costume to decorate the window surrounds and the spandrels between them. The building's height and its verticality are reinforced visually by engaged columns which draw the eye towards the undulating patterns of the gables and the stunning colours of the roof. These are capped by ceramic bee-hive forms while rows of ceramic bees rise in relief up the columns, representing thrift, saving and hard work, the virtues which the Postal Savings Bank aimed to encourage. The bees also represent a vision of the act of saving in a common store and of working together for the good of a larger system (i e the state) as something which pre-dates society; a notion already inherent in nature. If saving is a natural act, then it follows that it must be something programmed into us by instinct and consequently a higher power. This can be seen as a justification for the existence of the bank as an institution, it is merely accommodating a natural, pre-ordained desire and is not the unholy (un-Christian/Jewish) well of immorality and usurers.

Between the bee-hive capped columns lies an organically wavy series of gables adorned with flower motifs taken from folk embroidery and ceramics. These in turn are crowned with faience mouldings including odd, vegetable-shaped pinnacles and little wings. Beyond these spreads the vast expanse of the shimmering green roof. Whereas Wagner's bank was crowned by angels, Lechner adorned the ridges of his building with serpent's head motifs. The serpent, as mentioned earlier, is associated with the *caduceus* and thus with Mercury, patron of banking, and also with the energy and the cycle of life. Hens' heads, symbolising the treasure of the golden egg, provide another symbolic function when seen in conjunction with the snake; the hen protecting her young as the bank protects the savings of the meek. The rich roofscape culminates in three pinnacles at the centre and at either side of the main elevation, each capped by a delicate whirl of ceramic virtuosity and symbolism. The taller central pinnacle is crowned by a pair of bulls' heads based on the designs of those on a hoard of treasure which was then thought to have belonged to Attila the Hun. These would have represented a direct link with an ancient, semi-mythical Hungarian past but would have also symbolised the more straightforward function of representing the nation's treasure. In this way Lechner attempted to knit the building into national history and myth by using archetypes drawn from the collective unconscious of the nation. He was trying to develop an architecture which thrived on a deep connection to the Hungarian national spirit; the bank was to be the keep of the Hungarian castle, the place where national reserves would be built up to keep the country powerful.

Like Wagner's Postal Savings Bank, Lechner's building was organised around an impressive central banking hall lit from above, retaining an echo of the courtyards of the early exchanges. Whereas Wagner was to con-struct an elaborate two-tier system of glazing for his Vienna bank, Lechner's solution was simpler and, arguably despite its visual complexity, the more functional of the two.

The banking hall was surmounted by a lantern the sides of which were glazed and subdivided into undulating sections by organic mullions. The roof of the lantern was composed of thousands of small hexagonal, hollow glass blocks so that the effect, to continue the bee-hive metaphor, was rather like a honeycomb seen from within. Inside, the lantern was supported on columns and the crystalline dome sat on a clerestorey lighting system. Below the glass roof were benches, tables and fittings, all designed by Lechner in true *Gesamtkunstwerk* spirit; the lantern and fittings have all since been removed. Elsewhere, the building's interior continues with the themes and motifs introduced on the elevations; a curious mix of the functional and the symbolic. Modern materials are used throughout; cast-iron columns culminate in capitals depicting pigeons, hens and serpents, fruits, berries and flowers. Everywhere there are expansive windows giving natural light. The symmetrical plan, based around the central banking office with a pair of light-wells to either side and offices all around the perimeter of the building, is very close to Wagner's bank. Although the programmes and approaches of the two architects were strikingly different, the similarities are too many to ignore. Both created functional, rational buildings; Wagner's was decorated with bolts and cladding which made the building-as-machine metaphor manifestly readable, Lechner devoted his energy to a decorative scheme which would tie the bank into the Hungarian consciousness and make it a part of life. Wagner saw the building as a mechanism, it was the unsentimental efficiency of the building that was meant to assure savers that a new, reliable start was being made. Lechner too saw the building as a rational institution but attempted to see the bank as organism rather than machine, an organic masterpiece that could take its place in a mythical world which was perhaps more trustworthy than the cynical world of the international banks. Wagner's approach came to define the twentieth-century bank, Lechner's became extinct although arguably traces of its memory can be found in another remarkable Central European bank, Günther Domenig's Z-Bank in Graz.

THE MIDWESTERN BANKS
LOUIS H SULLIVAN

In the years between 1906 and 1920, Louis Sullivan, whose career had suffered a dramatic decline from what had been an almost pre-eminent position in U S architecture, built a series of eight banks in rural towns in the Midwest. This set of bank buildings is perhaps one of the most thoughtful additions to the oeuvre, as important in their own way as Soane's monumental work at the Bank of England or Wagner's severely rational Postal Savings Bank. Sullivan had made his name with a new urban type, the embryonic skyscraper. These were monumental buildings which defined a new era in American, and indeed European, architecture. He had become known as the formulator of that most iconic of Modernist dictums, 'Form follows Function'. Yet the nature of his major urban works, largely mixed-use buildings which needed to accommodate a wide variety of functions from shops to offices and banks, and the possibility that these functions would need to change, had created problems in the development of an architectural language capable of expressing the internal, rather than merely the structural, functions of the buildings. With the Midwestern banks Sullivan was able to explore a more specific and rigorous architectural, artistic and symbolic programme and effectively work towards his aim of creating an architecture which expressed the ideals of democracy and his personal vision of the American dream. As a place to formulate ideas about the development of a new American indigenous architecture, the small agricultural communities of the Midwest proved the ideal location. The genesis of these banks lies in a whole set of cultural and economic conditions which arose around the turn of the century and which changed the nature of banking in the United States .

In the rural Midwest banking was seen as a conspiracy by the East Coast, monopolies to limit the supply of money; an evil empire determined to get its claws into the hardworking agricultural base which lay at the heart of America's abundant wealth. Indeed farmers found it hard to get loans, which were needed particularly at harvest time to pay for machinery and labour costs, as the large national banks were unwilling to lend using agricultural land as collateral. The depression which swept the country in the 1890s exacerbated these problems and increased the farmers' distrust of the bankers who were unwilling to loan them the money they needed. This distrust led to the growing success of local savings banks that were able to lend using land as collateral, were more sympathetic to the needs of farmers and began to break the grip of the East Coast national banks. Even these savings banks, however, had to charge heavy interest to repay their own loans and the banks were still seen as a necessary evil. At the turn of the century, bankers were forming themselves into an organised profession and they played an increasingly important role in the civic life of communities. Once the depression eased, the early years of the twentieth century proved abundant, crops were plentiful and the local savings banks began to flourish and make huge profits. The bankers were mindful of the need to be seen to be contributing to the burgeoning development of the towns. They needed to construct a new image of the bank as a welcoming public space at the heart of the town's economic life; an indispensable and pivotal structure which would enhance the townscape and the reputation of their own profession. The new model of the bank was to be a democratic space where rich and poor alike were welcome, as were women who were beginning to start savings accounts independently of their husbands, while children too were encouraged to start saving early. The bankers sought to depict the wealth which had been generated by a run of exceptional harvests as somehow being due to their own services. They began to set up advice centres and worked closely with farmers in determining which crops would yield the best profit and even set up agricultural exhibition stands within the bank buildings. Until this period many banks had merely occupied main street storefront premises, acting almost as a money shop and often in a building which contained other commercial, retail and office functions. This image was seen to be too modest; the banks wanted to make their presence felt in an architectural fashion as a fulcrum of the townscape.

These changes in attitude and philosophy by the banks together with the increasing wealth of the communities and the banks' own coffers led to the commissioning of a rash of new, purpose-built banks across the Midwest. Of these Louis Sullivan's were undoubtedly the most interesting and the most successful.

Sullivan had to reconcile many often diverging ideals in his architecture: the banks wanted to show off their new found wealth, yet they did not want to appear arrogant. They wanted to make a statement about their presence in the town, yet the bank should not be too grand or it would be seen as an alien intrusion which was quite the opposite of what was wanted. The bank should be based around an impressive interior which suited the dignity of the transaction and showed the wealth, stability and confidence of the institution yet it was to be a space in which people could feel welcome and not intimidated. The provincial bank was to prove the ultimate test of Sullivan's aim to create a democratic American architecture. The first of Sullivan's bank buildings was also perhaps the best and perfectly demonstrates the sociological and economic conditions from which all the subsequent banks arose. The National Farmers' Bank in Owatonna, Minnesota (1906-08) is a grand piece of monumental architecture, which has found its way into the contemporary histories of modern architecture. In Owatonna Sullivan managed

National Farmers' Bank, Owatonna, 1906-08

to create a new prototype for the rural bank. Helped by an enlightened and daring client (the architect was, after all, seen to be on the way out at this stage in his career), Sullivan created a new architecture which was both an extension of and a corollary to his innovative skyscraper designs which had defined the last years of Modernist architectural histories of the nineteenth century. He also proved that his design approach was eminently applicable to rural as well as urban building types. Sullivan's master-stroke was to create a monumental architecture which did not derive its power from its scale but from its bold articulation. The National Farmers' Bank is a solid brick cube which rises from the town's grid plan thereby taking its form from the topology of the town itself and not appearing an alien object superimposed on it. Despite Sullivan's penchant and renown for organic decoration, the bank is defined simply by its tectonic elements: the solidity of the brick cube; the imposing openness of the grand, almost Roman arched openings; the solid and secure stone plinth upon which it stands; and the tripartite division of the building into vertical sections i e base, central section and cornice.

The bank's layout illustrates the beginnings of Sullivan's working towards the 'democratic' bank plan. Entry is through a small, confined lobby which emphasises the great expanse of the brilliantly lit main banking hall which follows it in the entry sequence. The location of the Farmers' Exchange Room and the President's Office on either side of the public entrance lobby is a firm gesture towards openness and democracy in the plan. Sullivan's ultimate ideal of the vault as the open and very public culmination of the plan was not yet realised with the design of this building. The client had stipulated a more closed system which entailed a pair of decorative grids over the tellers' windows that precluded the possibility of a straight through view. However, the secure door of the vault remains visible on the building's main central axis at the centre of the

great arch which forms the central feature of the end wall. Its preciousness, secure behind a brick structure housing the tellers' facilities, brings to mind a ritual progression towards a holy grail.

I began this book with an ecclesiastical analogy and at this point it is worth resurrecting that architectural metaphor. Sullivan saw the bank as a venue for an almost ritualistic experience, a series of revelations which culminated in the handing out of money, an act which could be seen as analogous in some curious way to receiving the host of communion. The vault in his buildings occupies the same position as would the high altar; if ever there was a confirmation of Heine's dictum about money being the religion of modernity, then it can be found in these buildings. It is also worth noting that America was seen both from inside and from outside as the land of capitalism. These buildings coincide with the revolutions in Russia and with the rise of Marxism as a force in Europe. They are built as bastions of money, strongholds at the heart of American small-town life. On a secular main street in a capitalist world the bank attempts to compete with the church as the pre-eminent building of social interaction, of awe and splendour, and as the repository of advice and of wisdom. Bearing this imagery in mind, it is paradoxical that Sullivan's aim was to 'democratise' the world of banking. To evoke architecturally the mystical ritual of the Christian liturgy would seem to be the least appropriate approach for bringing banking closer to the people, yet curiously there were architectural parallels in the ecclesiastical world which help to clarify the seeming paradox between a quasi-religious mystification of the banking ritual and the notion of opening out the financial world to the layman.

Modern architects and theologians had been working towards new visions of the function of the church building: the turn of the century saw a massive upheaval in architectural ideas based on a desire to demystify the ritual and lessen the gap between clergy and laity. Two of the most advanced and interesting ecclesiastical buildings of the early twentieth century can serve as paradigms here: Frank Lloyd Wright's Unity Temple in Oak Park, Illinois and Otto Wagner's Kirche am Steinhof in Vienna, both of which were completed in 1907. Wright, of course, had been Sullivan's most famous pupil and had taken much with him from his *Liebermeister*'s architectural approach and theorising. By the time Sullivan began building the Midwestern banks his former pupil had begun to outshine him and, perhaps more in Europe than in the USA, had become a pivotal influence in the development of modern architecture. Otto Wagner was an exact contemporary of Sullivan's and had formulated a similar philosophy of 'Form follows Function'; he had a substantially more dramatic effect on bank architecture with his Postal Savings Bank than Sullivan ever achieved, but if we think for a moment of his church in Vienna we see similar things going on to those we can see in Sullivan's banks. A rigidly axial church, pragmatic and functional, the design of a non-believer who saw the building in purely functional terms, the interior was well lit, logical and spacious, the altar was not separated from the congregation with rood-screens or the other trappings of mystification. The structure was massive, almost Byzantine in its grandeur, and it was the culmination of the tradition of the *Gesamtkunstwerk,* or total work of art, which was the grail of the Vienna Secession; the idea of a building in which all the arts are unified. In the banks Sullivan attempted the same thing, the buildings were conceived in the 'Craftsman' tradition with built-in Arts and Crafts furniture and fittings, decorated with mosaics and murals and the architect's signature organic iron and terracotta ornament. Frank Lloyd Wright was ambitiously aiming for a new spatial conception in his Unity Temple where the space enclosed becomes the architecture, it is a rather oriental notion of the architecture as the space rather than the shell. Importantly, it was also to be a meeting place

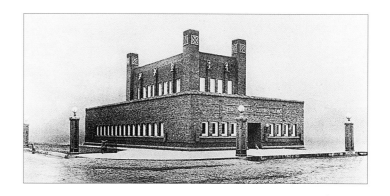

TOP and CENTRE: Peoples Savings Bank, Cedar Rapids, 1910
BOTTOM: Land and Loan Office, Algona, 1913

ABOVE: Merchants National Bank 1913-15, detail of entrance
CENTRE: Peoples Savings and Loan Association, 1916-18
BELOW: Peoples Savings and Loan Association, design

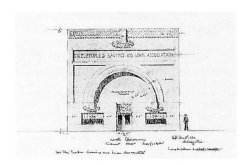

where people could come together and simply celebrate being, it was a temple to Man as much as to God. The ideas of both Wagner and Wright are to be found in the work of Sullivan and it is fair to say that their work was part of a general *Zeitgeist*, that there was cross-fertilisation and that the ideals of bank architecture and church architecture were curiously but undeniably linked. Looking at individual buildings, this becomes clearer.

The National Farmers' Bank in Owatonna laid the foundations for the resurrection of Sullivan's flagging career and his subsequent important commissions were limited exclusively to the world of banking. His architecture represented an American alternative to the Classicism which had dominated bank design throughout the Western world in the early twentieth century. The clients who commissioned buildings from Sullivan were making a bold gesture, these were still unconventional buildings despite the success of the National Farmers' Bank. The Peoples Savings Bank in Cedar Rapids, Iowa (1910-11) was a very different type of building. With a much lower budget than the building in Owatonna, Sullivan refined his ideas about a democratic plan in a far more functional shell. Although still decorated with the architect's characteristic organic motifs, this was an austere little structure, the simplicity of its open interior expressed eloquently in the massing and the stark cubic volumes. The hard, pressed brick of the elevations gives way to marble and murals within following broadly the same sequence as the plan of the Owatonna bank, ie low, tight lobby followed by expansive double-height banking hall and tellers and vaults ahead on the main axis. The ecclesiastical analogy is clear in the processional nature of the route and the arrangement of the plan into a nave and side aisles, a clerestorey and the tellers at the high altar behind the rood-screen of the grilles. These are lighter thus allowing a greater visual route from end to end. Despite the building's stark exterior the colour scheme inside revealed Sullivan's sophisticated Impressionist palate, greens and yellows in the marble, blue leaded glass windows in the clerestorey and a yellow skylight were meant to suggest the colours of the open prairie, the green expanses of grass, the yellow of the corn and the blue of the sky. In fact Sullivan's use of colour in his bank buildings was perhaps the most sophisticated and considered of all his contemporaries.

Sullivan's success in Cedar Rapids led to a rash of commissions from impressed, economy conscious bankers in other towns in Iowa. The long, narrow site for the Land and Loan Office in Algona (1913-14) necessitated a departure from Sullivan's favoured arrangement with the vault as high altar; an asymmetrical plan was adopted with the vault at its heart. The elevations were once again austere and powerfully geometrical with thick brick walls. The Purdue State Bank in West Lafayette, Indiana (1914-15) followed a similar pattern but was adapted to a free-standing site. The Merchants National Bank in Grinnel, Iowa, the design of which was contemporary with the last two banks allowed Sullivan a freer rein in decoration. The ecclesiastical metaphor is powerfully resurrected by the highly decorated main entrance above which is placed an elaborate rose window surrounded by the architect's characteristic organic foliate designs. These combine the motifs of the geometry of the square and the circle with the botanical decoration, suggesting that Sullivan is attempting to reconcile the mechanical rigour of building with the transcendental beauty of nature. The building's interior was simple, refined and reminiscent of the work of Sullivan's old draughtsman, Frank Lloyd Wright. The interior of the Home Building Association, Newark, Ohio (1914-15) was a comparative sunburst of colour and rich material. Veined marble covered all the surfaces while the upper level and ceiling of the double-height interior was adorned with

polychromatic abstract patterns. The plan is exquisitely simple and democratic in the architect's own terminology, a simple corridor of space with windows and seats along one side and tellers' desks along the other. The thin front elevation was also covered in brilliantly coloured pattern and foliate relief. His next design, the Peoples Savings and Loan Association, Sidney, Ohio (1916-18), saw a return to some of the forms of the Owatonna bank; the architect regarded it as his finest bank building.

The bank's monumental exterior and the grand Byzantine arch give access to a stripped down interior, open, light and without the fussiness of earlier designs. The interior culminated in a view of the great door of the vault and is perhaps the high-point of his search for a democratic plan. The building was the perfect response to war-time economies, minimal and restrained; Sullivan managed to retain a human scale and a minimum of decoration which is never intrusive or distracting. The building also included a series of technical innovations in ventilation and insulation, as did all Sullivan's other banks and, in fact, they proved highly adaptable to new technologies of air-conditioning and computerisation, unlike many buildings constructed much later. The Farmers and Merchants Union Bank in Columbus, Wisconsin (1919), the architect's final bank building followed a similar pattern and is reminiscent of the stripped brick architecture which was becoming popular in Holland and Germany at the same time. The decoration was increasingly confined to the main facade, the bank's interior was the simplest yet, a functional, brightly lit hall which has perhaps never been surpassed as a model of provincial banking architecture. Sullivan's legacy is remarkable, no other single architect has done so much to create an oeuvre in the field of bank architecture and his buildings remain as models of thoughtful and far-sighted building for banks.

THE TWENTIETH CENTURY

The bank which paved the way for developments in the twentieth century more than any other was undoubtedly Wagner's Post Office Savings Bank. In one of Europe's most self-consciously monumental and grand capital cities, Wagner succeeded in creating a new banking prototype: a light, airy structure, uncluttered with ornament and decoration with a clear rational plan and construction. It was a transparent building in that the effect was more of a greenhouse or an exhibition pavilion than the traditional image of the solidity of a bank. Even the vaults, traditionally the one part of the bank which could not be subverted and that had to be seen as strong and inaccessible, were placed beneath the glass floor. It is a building opened up to the public, Wagner's cutaway perspective of the building which shows it in elevation and section is a fine illustration of the idea of a building enclosing an interior which remains part of the public realm, more like a great courtyard than a forbiddingly massive bank strong-room. With its open, public character it was a logical and small step to Skidmore Owings and Merrill's Manufacturer's Hanover Trust Company building in New York built half a century later in 1954. That building confirmed the shift of the centre of innovation in bank architecture from Europe to the USA, a process which had been steadily gaining pace for the last couple of decades and which was accelerated by the devastation and the debt incurred by the European countries after the Second World War. Wagner's Post Office Savings Bank, brilliant and strikingly original as it was, did not have the immediate architectural impact which one might suspect. Its departure from the traditional language of financial architecture, from the conservative solidity and heavy rustication which were familiar from banks throughout the world, was too sudden and too radical. The period directly before the First World War and the years which followed it were dominated by conservatism and the impact of Modernism was in fact far less powerful than is often reported; and nowhere was the impact of Modernism less impressive than in the architecture of banks. London remained the world's banking and communications capital in the years directly before and after the First World War; its geographical position between the USA and Europe and its political position as the hub of a great empire made it an ideal commercial centre, although in terms of wealth and industrial pre-eminence it was being rapidly overtaken by the USA. The building boom of the turn of the century continued after the First World War and was finally slowed down by the depression of the 1930s. Building acts set a maximum height for buildings and steel framing appeared much later on the British building scene than it had done in the USA; these factors combined with innate British reluctance to address change and the particular conservatism of the banking sector led to a very different set of buildings to those rising in the American cities which we will examine later. Sir Herbert Baker's massive and dull rebuilding of the Bank of England (1921-39) largely set the scene for a huge programme of London bank building between the wars, big, impressive buildings with often spectacular banking halls and Modernism nowhere to be seen. Sir Edwin Lutyens' Midland Bank (1924-39), which took inspiration from the form of an aqueduct, spanned the same period as Baker's Bank of England and represented the restrained and impressive, if conservative, style of Britain's establishment architect *par excellence*. Edwin Cooper's National Provincial Bank (1929-31), Mewè's and Davis' London County and Westminster Bank (1921-32) and Sir John Burnet's Lloyds Bank (1927-30) set the tone for other bank architects while an American Beaux Arts influence and a restrained Neo-Georgian also appeared at this time. Many of the banking halls survive as a testament to an era when solidity, conservatism and a desire to impress constituted the architectural language of the banks. If the banks' headquarters proved immune to the influence of modern architecture, the architects of the branches were often able to accommodate elements of the new aesthetic developments. Art Deco and *moderne* influences appeared in a number of branch offices; Edward Maufe's Lloyds Bank in Putney (1927-28) and W F C Holden's National Provincial Bank in Osterley (1936), both in London, are good examples.

In the USA the development of the skyscraper, an apparently resolutely modern building type, did not lead to an immediate triumph of modern architecture, but it dominated the designs of the big banks in the major cities. The introduction of elevators, electric light and steel-framing together made possible the modern tall building with much deeper floors now that natural light was not the dominant principle. But many architects were unsure how to handle the form and resorted to placing a tall shaft upon a Classical base. McKim Mead and White's design for the National City Bank in New York of 1909 is the perfect illustration of the inability to address the new building form even though Sullivan had begun to lay out some fundamental principles in his own work in the previous century. New York's 1920 zoning laws which governed rules about light in the city began to suggest the stepping-back of large buildings, the architectural effects of which were brilliantly mapped out in Hugh Ferris' visionary drawings. In conjunction with the growing fascination with the pyramidal forms of Egypt, inspired by Howard Carter's remarkable discoveries, and of native American cultures, the familiar stepped Art Deco forms began to appear. Art Deco itself was seen as too flash for the banks and although some details and shapes may have been influenced by the style, it never really took off. Halsey, McCormick and Helmer's Williamsburg Savings

ABOVE: E Maufe, Lloyds Bank, London 1927-28 CENTRE and BELOW: Halsey, McCormick and Helmer, Williamsburgh Savings Bank Tower, New York, 1929

ABOVE and BELOW: PSFS Building, Philadelphia

Bank Tower (1929) is a fine example of the bank as skyscraper. It is an oddly eclectic building, yet remains imposing and powerful projecting an effect of impressive gravitas and mass from its stone-clad base to its domed clock tower. With land values in the big American cities soaring in the post-war boom, and staying high even in the ensuing depression, the idea of the skyscraper, a huge block of rentable office space above the shop, appealed to the banks and became the only feasible option if a substantial site was sought. In a way this led to the decline of the bank as a building type. From now on banks in major city centres would invariably become a mix of office and financial functions which diluted the power of the building as a single, corporate statement. On the other hand it saw the major bank buildings becoming a vertical statement of power and wealth, a factor which has become and remains critically important.

The one building which stood out in the inter-war years as a sign of things to come was the Philadelphia Saving Fund Society headquarters building by George Howe and William Lescaze (1926-32). Remarkably, George Howe had been educated in the Beaux Arts tradition and had spent the early part of his career designing historicising suburban houses. His partner, William Lescaze, however, had had more experience of the avant-garde and the emergent International Style through his Swiss background. Although other American architects had begun to incorporate motifs from the European Modern Movement into their large office buildings, often toned down with Art Deco details and streamlining, the PSFS Building was the first skyscraper to be conceived as a unified Modernist statement. It is interesting to note that the building was completed in the year in which the Museum of Modern Art in New York held its historic exhibition on the 'International Style' (ie European Modernism) and it demonstrates just how far ahead Howe and Lescaze were within the American avant-garde.

George Howe and William Lescaze spent years refining a new approach to tall buildings; each aspect of the PSFS Building was considered in detail and integrated into the whole. Perhaps the only other significant designs which had envisaged such a radical, rational approach to the problem of tall buildings came directly from the Bauhaus; Hannes Meyer's design for the League of Nations building in Geneva (1927) and two entries to the Chicago Tribune Building Competition of 1922, the joint design of Walter Gropius and Adolf Meyer and that of Knut Lonberg-Holm. All of these designs were unsuccessful in com-petition and none was built. Howe and Lescaze's building was in many ways more daring than any of these; this was a building which followed through the strict ideals of Functionalism in a way which few architects have since managed. The lower part of the building housed shops and access from the subway as the building is situated in the middle of a busy commercial and retail district. The hope was that a well-located shopping centre, housing prestigious retailers, would attract the type of clientele the bank was aiming for. It was a subtle exercise in drawing people into a building and one which has been largely forgotten since. The main banking floor was raised and reached via an escalator in a striking and radical departure from the norm. It was as if the great height of the building elevated its function, raising it up to another level. This elevation of the function was further emphasised by the fine marble and chrome which were used to finish the surfaces and by the large window which curved slickly around the corner in a gesture of reconciliation to the street. Offices for rental were placed in the tower. Light, airy and, unusually for this period, air-conditioned, these too were rational and modern. The horizontality of the strip windows of the offices was balanced by the dark, vertical mass of the service core and by a series of piers which rises through the full height of the tower drawing the eye towards the sky. The building was crowned by the initials PSFS defined in huge red neon letters. At the time it was still not customary to use initials in place of a company's full name and these four red letters, which can be seen from all over the city and beyond, are a fine early example of the evolution of the building as corporate logo, an iconic sign. The building was a success but it proved too revolutionary. It still stands as a monument to the foresight of the bank's

president, James L Willcox, who was not deterred from commissioning a building which constituted such a break from tradition within the notoriously conserva-tive world of banking. It was to be another two decades before the consequences of Modernism in the architecture of banking, anticipated by this building, were truly realised.

In the years between the wars revolution, depression, Socialism and Communism all threatened to topple, or at least question, the basis of capitalism. In such an unstable climate, architectural conservatism was a logical reaction and mild Historicism and Eclecticism became entrenched as the unassailable approaches for the architecture of finance. This is not to say that fine buildings were not produced, rather, that this book explores the evolution of Modernism in bank architec-ture. Thus, the banks designed and erected in Britain between the wars, those in Nazi Germany and Fascist Italy as well as elsewhere, although often architecturally impressive, must be left out of this narrative. It is perhaps surprising then that a handful of buildings which are of more interest to us from this period does not come from one of these bastions of monetarism and international capital but from the Soviet Union. The explosion of visionary schemes for the construction of the new Soviet Union after the devastation of war and civil war included a number of remarkable designs for banks, many exactly contemporary with Howe and Lescaze's designs for the Philadelphia Savings Fund Society building.

Vladimir Krinsky's design for the skyscraper head-quarters of the Supreme Soviet of the National Economy (1923) is so striking that it remains almost shocking retaining an iconoclastic power which has not yet been equalled, although its skewed, layered grids can be seen adopted as a symbolic gesture in many recent designs. If this was to have been the centre of the Soviet banking world, it would have set the stage for a revolution in banking architecture; other dramatic designs did follow and some were executed. Viktor Vesnin's Ivselbank Agricultural Bank was realised in 1927, a powerful, blocky asymmetric mass which was both solid yet open to the public realm through a ground floor of glass. Grigorii Barkhin's competition-winning design for the State Bank in Novisibirsk (1929) was a similar exercise in Constructivist massing on a much larger scale, a bold play of solid and void which recalled the dynamism of Iakov Chernikov's architectural fantasies. Ilya Golosov's design for the Elektrobank (1926) was a bold, rational block with a pure Platonic solidity; its most striking feature was the cylindrical glass stair tower which also formed the main entrance and which appeared in a more sophisticated version the following year at his Moscow Workers' Club building. Georgi Golts' and Alexander Shvidovsky's design for a bank in the same city (1926) displayed a rigorous, clean functionalism. Yet, despite the exuberance of these designs, at the height of Constructivism in the Soviet avant-garde, an extension to the State Bank in Moscow (1927-29) was built in a rather flat, Renaissance style which recalled the cool control of Alberti. The architect, Ivan Zholtovsky, who was helped in the design by his student Georgi Golts, stuck by his Classical principles and was censured by the leading Constructivists for doing so. Although as an addition to an existing Classical building (dating from 1895) this was a successful if unspectacular construction it is interesting to compare it with its exact contemporary, Herbert Baker's competently dull rebuilding of the Bank of England, even if it would be hard to find two more different circumstances for a banking commission.

In the 1930s, the worldwide depression put a harsh stop to the building of flagship banks and to the commissioning of more radical architects so that, throughout Europe and the USA, few noteworthy banks were built or designed. Among the few exceptions was Hans Poelzig's design for a new Reichshauptbank in Berlin (1932). This imposing gasometer of a building would have created a powerful symbol and made a confident statement for the German bank in the midst of the economic crisis. Based on a type of panopticon plan, the building revolved around a central, circular hall and a large circular lobby which prepared the visitor for the round theme and took them up a monumental staircase. A ring of offices made up the circumference of the building and within were the archives and vaults. If it had been built, Poelzig's design would undoubtedly have been one of the most influential and staggering bank buildings of the century, but the gradual rise of Hitler saw Poelzig's elemental architecture, with its powerfully and still visibly Expressionist roots, fall out of favour.

Like the First World War, the Second World War had a devastating effect on the European economies and, as after the First World War, the USA emerged all-powerful, buoyed by sales of arms, machinery and goods and untouched by the physical devastation which had scarred the European continent and Japan. The economic and architectural climate in the USA was utterly changed in the wake of the war; the corporations and banks had become even wealthier, more powerful and influential in the life of the great American cities. The drive for grandeur and jazzy decoration which characterised the best of 1930s corporate architecture was replaced by a greater emphasis on economy and efficiency, an almost mechanistic vision of society. Buildings began to change radically: partly due to a lack of craftsmen capable of executing the delicate work involved in Art Deco decoration; partly due to a need to construct air-conditioned, efficient downtown offices on a huge scale; and partly to economy and a new aesthetic vision. The post-war bank building developed into an almost completely new building type, albeit one which had been presaged by Howe and Lescaze's Philadelphia Savings Fund Society building. Another factor which contributed significantly to the new developments in corporate architecture was a change to the New York building regulations which had hitherto insisted on the stepping back of tall buildings to meet light requirements for the street. The revisions meant that if the tall part of a building was set back from the street at its base, creating the now much disliked archetype of the windswept plaza in front, then it could be constructed as a solid slab. Equally important in the development of the new architecture was the arrival in the USA of the Bauhaus architects whom Tom Wolfe sarcastically named the 'White Gods' for the awed reverence in which they were held by their American hosts. Walter Gropius and Marcel

Breuer exerted a powerful influence on young American architects but it was Mies van der Rohe who cast the longest shadow on American design. His Seagram Building in New York, designed with his apostle Philip Johnson (1954-58), became a model for almost all corporate architecture. The Seagram Building was the ultimate realisation of the all-glass skyscraper which had obsessed Mies since the 1920s and it can be seen as the fulfilment of the Expressionist dream of the crystal mountain as a new world image, the mystical image of the cosmos as a construction of crystal and glass radiating a heavenly light. The corporate New York skyscraper seems a long way from that mystical-Socialist fantasy yet the development took place well within the span of Mies' active career. It is a testament to the dramatic speed at which the aesthetics of modern architecture were changing and to the ability of the corporate capitalist establishment to absorb and assimilate the avant-garde to suit its own needs.

European Modernism had already exerted a significant influence on American architecture before Mies' skyscraper was realised. It was the banks that led the way in adapting the new aesthetic to major urban buildings. If Lescaze's PSFS Building in the conservative city which had been home to the founding fathers, Philadelphia, laid the foundations of avant-garde Modernist office design in the USA, it was an Italian immigrant, Pietro Belluschi, who realised the first building of the next generation in his Equitable Savings and Loan Association Building on the other side of the country, in Portland, Oregon (1944-48). Belluschi's exquisite, smooth building remains a startlingly modern structure. It was not set back from the building line as were so many of the later Modernist blocks, instead, it accentuated the direction and the dynamic of the street. The expansive green glass is contained within a grid, the whole surface almost flush so that the building retains an unprecedented purity. The asymmetry of Howe and Lescaze's PSFS Building is replaced by a confident evenness throughout the elevations, the smooth and shiny surfaces reflect the sky and the clouds in an ethereal illusion of weightlessness. This was an altogether different image of the bank,

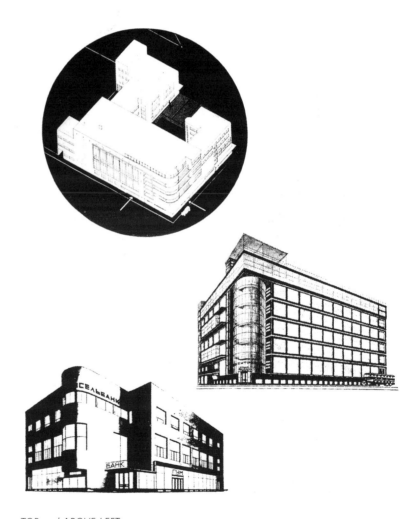

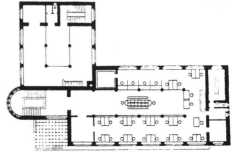

TOP and ABOVE LEFT: Grigorii Barkhin, Design for State Bank, Novisibirsk,1929 CENTRE: Ilya Golosov, Design for Electrobank, Moscow 1926 LEFT and RIGHT: Viktor Vesnin, Design for Ivselbank, Ivanovo-voznesensk, 1927, perspective and plan

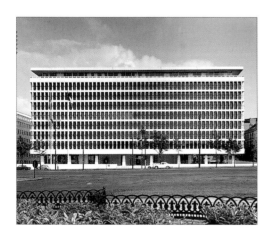

TOP: Hans Poelzig, Design for the Reichshauptbank, Berlin, 1932
CENTRE: SOM, Manufacturers Hanover Trust, New York, 1953-54
BOTTOM: SOM, Banque Bruxelles Lambert, 1964

transparent, democratic and self-effacingly minimal. The next important building made this fundamental change even more apparent, Skidmore, Owings and Merrill's Manufacturers Hanover Bank (1953-54), a building which saw the momentum in modern bank design move back to New York once more. Designed a little less than a decade later than Belluschi's building, SOM used a harsher architecture, less smooth but equally slick. The Manufacturers Hanover Bank represented the most important step in modern bank architecture since Wagner's Postal Savings Bank in Vienna half a century earlier. As SOM were heavily influenced by the work and the architectonic language of Mies van der Rohe, it could be argued that this development too stemmed from Europe, but perhaps that would be a little simplistic as it is in the context of its Fifth Avenue address which this building needs to be seen.

The fundamental idea of the building can be seen as the ultimate realisation of Wagner and Sullivan's democratisation of the architectural manifestation of the banking process; this is a completely open building. Sullivan had attempted to make the bank vault the culmination of a ritual route, both visual and physical, within the bank. I have compared the vault to a high altar within a church, a gateway to a mystical realm, and his bank buildings are often compared to jewel boxes betraying their precious contents through their architecture. In the Manufacturers Hanover Trust Company building, however, the architects developed this idea a stage further by opening out the bank to the street; fully glazed and fully transparent the building achieves what Wagner's Post Office Savings Bank had achieved in a cut-away perspective drawing only: complete openness to the public realm.

The building was arranged on four floors with a suite of penthouse offices set back from the building line. In proportional composition it remained a Classical design with a large basement housing the conspicuous round stainless steel door of the vault so that pedestrians looked into the heart of the bank's operations. Above, was a *piano nobile*, the grandest of the levels with the highest ceiling height, the floor of which was set back from the facade. These two lower storeys accommodated the banking halls and the public parts of the building, the floors being linked by escalators, and they were surmounted by two levels of offices plus the attic storey of penthouse accommodation. By sticking to a relatively low-rise building with an almost Renaissance elevational system the bank is advertising its prestige. It is as if they do not need to build high to make more money, it is more important to have a dignified *palazzo* of a building. More importantly, however, the bank opened up a display to the public realm. This is Fifth Avenue, the heart of commercial and retail New York, the bank is presenting a shop window to exhibit the world of money. This was a critical *volte-face* in banking architecture which had traditionally presented a dignified but closed world to the public. Now the bank was presenting itself as a service, with a prestigious window display to match those of the downtown department stores. It was the beginning of a very great change in attitudes to design.

SOM built on the outstanding success of the Manufacturers Hanover Bank with a series of important and influential buildings which for the ensuing couple of decades made them the almost unchallenged leaders in the field. The Chase Manhattan Bank, also in New York (1957-61), retained some of the openness and transparency of the Manufacturers Hanover Bank but was capped with an enormous, if elegant, Miesian glass box. This was in the style of their highly influential Lever House, New York, 1952 but the extra structure required entailed a loss of the immediacy and closeness to the street which their previous bank had so successfully achieved. The Banque Bruxelles Lambert (1964) represented a move away from the glass box, a reinforced concrete structure made up of a repeated grid of prismatic elements and the usual Modernist plaza. Other large banks followed: the First City National Bank, Houston, Texas, (1959-61) and the Bank of America, San Francisco (1969), which saw a departure from the Miesian glass box to an elevation articulated by a series of angular bays, the modelling of which began almost heretically to recall the geometric patterns of Art Deco. In the 1970s SOM seemed to lose

their edge and settled into a pattern of bland offices including the Ohio National Bank, Columbus, Ohio (1976), which summed up an era in which the glass box became the *lingua franca* of untalented corporate architects and a symbol of a lack of imagination among both clients and designers.

The 1970s did, however, produce a number of interesting departures from the faceless glass box which disfigures so many of the world's financial districts. The decade began with Gunnar Birkerts' design for the Federal Reserve Bank of Minneapolis, Minnesota (1971-73). Here the dream of maximum unhindered floorspace was achieved in a building which was suspended on cables hung from structural supports at either end with a bridge at the top to stop the building being pulled apart. The curve of the cables is powerfully expressed on the elevations through a change in material defining a huge parabola.

Around the middle of the 1970s, shapes other than the rectangle and cube began to appear on buildings. Hugh Stubbins' Citicorp Center, New York (1973-78), was a perfectly pure block but with a chamfered top. The tower sits on a huge set of legs, rising through ten storeys, which allows the land at the base of the building to be occupied by shops and a public plaza as well as by an interesting, angular church. This was designed by Stubbins to replace the original building which was demolished to make way for the Citicorp Center. The building's pure articulation and simple continuous band windows are capped off with a chamfered top. Over the next few years the tops of buildings would provide much of the architectural interest as little innovation or originality went on elsewhere in the architecture. This striking roofline not only helps to define the building against the plethora of second-rate Miesian blocks which proliferates in downtown New York; it also houses a massive concrete block designed to reduce the sway of the skyscraper in high winds, an effect achieved through the utilisation of the block's inertia slowing down the building's response to wind. Thus the building's primary visual feature is determined (even if tenuously) by function rather than whimsy; this was soon to change.

POST-MODERNISM AND BEYOND

Capitalism, for better or for worse, has become the dominant world political and socio-economic system, unchallenged since the collapse of Soviet Communism. At the heart of capitalism is money. I began the book with an ecclesiastical metaphor, the bank as the cathedral of money. If any modern building type has taken the place of the cathedral as a symbol of what society strives for and aspires too, it is the modern bank headquarters building in the centre of the modern metropolis. The architectural manifestations of Post-Modernism and the changes which have occurred subsequently have restored the means for expression of the bank's dominance in contemporary culture. The post-war period was dominated by a Miesian architecture personified by the work of SOM which saw a homogenisation of all corporate building. With only a few exceptions, including SOM's own Hanover Manufacturers Trust Building, the architecture of banking lost its character as a recognisable oeuvre. This, after all, had been an architecture based on the principles of the Bauhaus and a group of Socialists and idealists, albeit ones who readily embraced American post-war culture when it held out its arms to their works. Post-Modernism, on the other hand, was a reaffirmation of the virtue of wealth and conspicuous consumption.

From the 1970s architects and clients began again to search for new tectonic languages to express the idea of the bank. New artistic impulses coincided with unprecedented changes in the banking industry which led to a radical rethinking of both the image and the functions which needed to be accommodated within the architecture of banking. Banks began to diversify into all the financial services and the traditional relationship of the customer to the banker was subtly but fundamentally changed. Although the bank had always maintained a presence in the commercial and retail districts of towns and cities it had traditionally been presented as something distinct from the shops. Banking was seen as a kind of quasi-mystical process which involved rituals and a set of formal relationships defined by strict codes of decorum and tradition. The great banking halls at the centre of these buildings were meant to inspire awe and to reinforce perceptions of banking as a somehow separate, mythical world with the vault at its heart, an unattainable holy grail of treasure. As has been shown, Sullivan and Wagner and later SOM were instrumental in breaking down the secrecy of the vault and opening up the inherently closed institution of the bank to the wider public realm. But throughout most of the twentieth century, despite the work of these pioneers, the contact between client and banker inevitably took place, as it has always done, over a physical barrier – the counter or the bank manager's desk. In the USA there was traditionally less formality than there was in Europe, and Britain in particular, but everywhere this kind of system formed the physical basis of banking.

Towards the end of the twentieth century this pivotal relationship between the customer and the banker was reassessed and this fundamental change helped to bring about a wholly new approach to the architecture of banks. This affected not only the design of the branch bank but reverberated through each stage in the hierarchy right through to the corporate banking headquarters, a cross section of which can be found in the later part of this book. Banks are now seen as part of the service industry which now dominates the post-industrial cities of the developed world. They have become more and more analogous to supermarkets rather than the aloof, semi-mystical, almost ecclesiastical spaces which they had been. Just as the supermarket has replaced the specialised high street shop, so the banks have diversified and offer a huge range of services to the customer in an increasingly informal atmosphere. At the same time information technology and computerisation have drastically altered the industry and the architecture which accommodates it. Telephone and Internet banking are growing rapidly, employees are housed in cheap, edge-of-town sheds which offer no real advances in architecture. Banks in town centres are increasingly becoming merely 'money shops' reminiscent of the portable booth set up at fairs where the money changer conducted his business with a minimum of backup. Now back-up services are also being moved to out-of-town locations to save on rent and drive towards efficiency, minimising the duplication of services in each branch. Some branches are now permanently unstaffed, all interaction is with a machine. Through cash dispensers and telephone operators, banking has become a twenty-four-hour facility and even the most complicated of transactions can be carried out on a computer or by telephone. In the UK the term for a public holiday is 'bank holiday' as it was thought too radical to propose a public holiday to employers keen to squeeze every last drop of labour from their downtrodden employees, Scrooge style. It is a measure of the dominance of banking that the term came to be applied nationally; when the bank stops working so does the nation. Now even bank holidays are not sacrosanct, many transactions can still be carried out even on holidays, further evidence of banking's shift into the service sector.

Architecturally these changes have led to a series of new building types within banking, although there is as yet little evidence of innovation in design to follow these momentous changes. In this book I have attempted to look broadly at the headquarters and major offices of a few large banking corporations but in these buildings too we can see signs of the changing nature of banking. In the period between the wars and

Gordon Bunshaft of SOM, National Commercial Bank, Jeddah, Saudi Arabia, 1981-83

directly after the architecture of banking in Europe and North America remained traditional, still based in the aesthetic tradition of the Renaissance. The banks, like the great Florentine families who were responsible for the rise of modern international banking, attempted to portray an image of solidity and permanence; to establish a presence in the heart of the major cities which would last and be seen to be grand, expensive and a public monument, yet paradoxically also to remain understated and secure. Around the middle of the century the glass box was adopted as the corporate symbol *par excellence* by the banks as well as by other major institutions. From the 1950s to the early 1970s this was virtually unquestioned, but in the 1970s shifts in architectural theory quickly affected bank architecture. The banks have always been in the unusual position of representing the heart of the establishment, the capitalist world order, yet also of being able to occasionally fund and commission the most expensive buildings from avant-garde architects who would be unable to execute their extravagant designs on a smaller budget. As these architects are often radical by their very nature the situation throws up a number of fascinatingly paradoxical buildings – certainly Günther Domenig's Z-Bank in Vienna and Behnisch Behnisch and Partner's Landesgirokasse in Stuttgart, both featured in later chapters, exemplify this trend. Generally, however, the banks seem to have been pleased with the advent of Post-Modernism and the subsequent reappraisal of Modernism in all its forms from High-Tech to the clean lines of Erick van Egeraat or John McAslan. The banks were among the first to commission landmark Post-Modern buildings and were instrumental in the development of the language of a Post- Modern architectural language. Arquitectonica's Banco de Credito in Lima (designed 1982) and Gordon Bunshaft of SOM's National Commercial Bank in Jeddah (1981-83) were among the early large-scale experiments in this emerging architec-

tural language. Bunshaft, along with his contemporary Philip Johnson, was responsible for defining the American corporate glass box after Mies van der Rohe. He was also one of the major figures to promote the forms of Post-Modern architecture which subverted the ethical and moral architectural ideals of Modernism.

The reasons for the enthusiasm with which the big banks embraced Post-Modernism can probably be explained by a few basic needs. Tom Wolfe has cynically described the capacity of grand, colourful and self-indulgent Post-Modernism to fill the void left by Corporate Modernism: undoubtedly the big banks were deprived of a distinctive means of artistic expression when the only acceptable type of building was the Miesian glass block. Like the Florentine dynasties, modern bankers wished to stamp their presence on the city but if all corporate architecture was to look the same, they would be unable to use architecture as a means of displaying corporate identity distinct from any other business. This leads us back to the idea of architecture as billboard. Banking is relatively hard to market through images so the architecture of its prestigious headquarters' buildings needs to take on the role of advertising the bank's desired image, be that one of conservatism, solidity or radicalism and openness to ideas and advances in technology. Once Robert Venturi had linked architecture to junk-culture images (Las Vegas neons, odd-shaped diners etc) architects and clients began to see buildings once more as distinctive forms which could visibly enhance the image of a corporation that would otherwise be perceived as bland or bureaucratically faceless. It was to prove a huge leap in architectural expression, leaving a trail of incompetent monstrosities and a few excellent buildings which paved the way for a radical renewal in built form.

Since the 1980s the big banks have remained among the most adventurous of corporate clients. Buildings like Ton Alberts' fantastic, organic masterpiece, the ING Bank in Amsterdam (1983-88) have shown a

ABOVE and LEFT: Carlo Scarpa, Banca Popolare di Verona, 1975, details

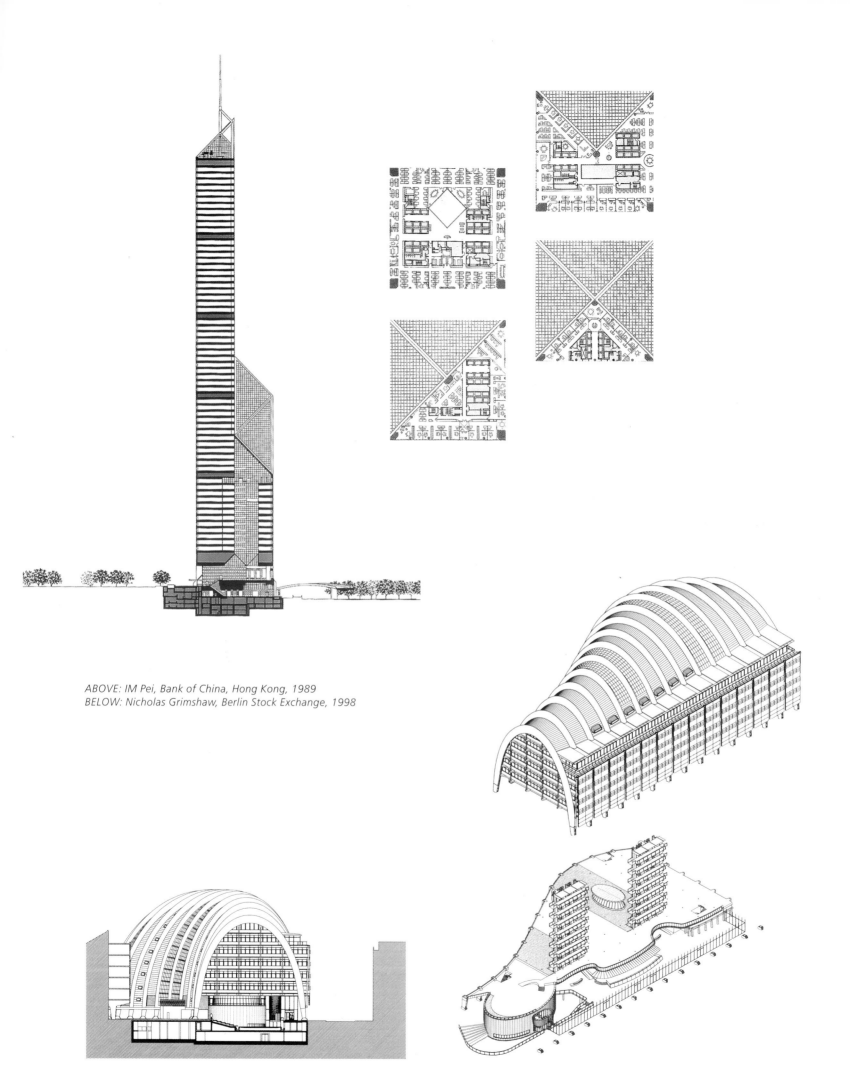

ABOVE: IM Pei, Bank of China, Hong Kong, 1989
BELOW: Nicholas Grimshaw, Berlin Stock Exchange, 1998

willingness to confront environmental issues in a way which is the diametric opposite of the glass box. Banks have also played a critical role in the urban landscape, one of the central ensemble of public buildings at the heart of towns and cities. Rationalisation, technology and big mergers have led to a reduction in the number of bank buildings needed on high-rent streets and squares and many fine buildings have been disappearing, or have had their uses changed and their interiors destroyed. A few landmark historical buildings have been conserved and restored, Swanke Hayden Connell's work at the Bowery Savings Bank in New York is a good example of what can be achieved. Other architects have turned their attention to the creation of new small buildings which enhance the cityscape. Carlo Scarpa led the way in this field with a couple of fine, thoughtful works: the exquisitely detailed Banca Popolare di Verona in Verona (1973-80) and the Banca Popolare di Gemona in Gemona (1978). Other architects (some featured here) are also addressing conservation and urbanistic issues in their buildings and it is refreshing to see the wealth of the banks put to these uses rather than merely as an expression of their power.

At the other end of the scale, the skyscraper too has made a comeback in bank design. With the demise of Miesian Modernism as the corporate design ideology, sculptural elements are back in vogue and the potential of the city-centre skyscraper as corporate symbol has been realised to a greater degree than at any time since the 1930s. As banks merge to create more and more powerful and influential organisations, and as new financial capitals are created in Europe, the USA and in Asia, the urge to assert identity becomes increasingly dominant and can be seen expressed in recent buildings, Norman Foster's Commerzbank in Frankfurt and his Hongkong and Shanghai Bank, I M Pei's Bank of China (also in Hong Kong) and Kohn Pederson Fox's DG Bank in Frankfurt are perhaps the best recent examples of this trend. These buildings become symbols not only of the banks but also of the cities they are in. The reunification of Germany is symbolised by the revitalisation of Berlin, its centre crowded with new financial buildings. These include Frank Gehry's DG Bank, Von Gerkan Marg and Partner's Dresdner Bank and Nicholas Grimshaw's new stock exchange, which has become a symbol of the city's revival as a trading centre on the European stage. The use of international architects is also instrumental in attempts to bring the city into the world arena from its previously provincial status as the divided ex-capital. Urban regeneration schemes in docklands areas in both London and New York have relied on banks to lead the way; Norman Foster's Citibank in London's Canary Wharf and Minoru Yamasaki's World Trade Centre in New York's Battery Park area (completed 1973) are examples.

Despite a series of financial disasters which have struck at the end of the twentieth century, global capitalism together with its stalwart guardians, the banks, has survived. Some of the worst, most conservative and least inspiring architecture of the century has been created by banks yet at the same time some of the best, most radical and most intelligent architecture of the century has relied on the financial might of the banks for its creation and this pattern reaches back to the beginning of the century as has been illustrated in the sections on pioneer bank architects. Banking remains a lively and important part of the world of architecture; it acts as a barometer to establish trends and fashions, to indicate contemporary concerns and political ideology (or the lack of it) and the state of world architecture itself. The mass of the city-centre bank headquarters is one of the finest markers we have of contemporary culture, simultaneously representing all that is good and all that is bad about the state of architecture and the state of the world economy. The bank is a hugely powerful architectural symbol and, for better or for worse, among the pre-eminent monuments of our age.

*The **ING Bank**, Amsterdam, 1983-88*

ALBERTS AND VAN HUUT

The ING Bank (formerly NMB Bank) in Amsterdam (1983-88) is a truly pioneering bank building in which the architects and the clients attempted fundamentally to address the traditional notion of the bank complex as a high-consumption, extravagant city-centre successor to the Renaissance palace; a corporate symbol designed to display wealth, power and the domination of the city. The architects also managed to resolve a number of seemingly incompatible problems which have traditionally faced bank architects in a manner which has led to a complete rethinking (in some quarters at least) of the architecture of corporate culture.

The building is located in a newly built suburb of Amsterdam rather than in the city centre and it houses a huge number of staff over an area which would have been inconceivable in an expensive downtown location. To give an idea of the scale of the project, it was built to house over 2,500 staff, is serviced by 350 metres of walkways linking the various elements and it includes four restaurants and a small theatre. The building is composed of a chain of individual elements arranged in a snaking S-shaped plan with each element linked to its neighbours. The huge mass of the building and the solidity of the battered walls evoke the image of a bastion, a fortified complex on a positively medieval scale. In keeping with the metaphor of the medieval castle wall, the buildings are arranged as a series of massive towers which could have the defensive advantage of good views all round and of protecting each other but are in fact planned to provide a maximum amount of natural light to the building's inhabitants. The architects have opted not for the walls of glass which are popular with bank architects as they allow light penetration into deep floor plates, but for a solution of traditional individual windows. This has the visual effect of increasing the bulk of the building but within the offices are meticulously planned in such a way that no worker is ever further than 7 metres from a window, a view and fresh air.

The small windows and massive walls are instrumental in maintaining a steady environmental climate within the building. Unlike the glass towers which became the norm for corporate headquarters from the 1950s, this building does not overheat in the summer or let all the heat escape in winter. The building's mass helps both to retain heat and stop massive solar gain in turn. It is naturally ventilated throughout: glazed roof-spaces create warm air which is subsequently circulated around the building in cold weather, in hot weather they act also to gather warm air from around the building whence it is expelled through vents. In section the unbroken route of the air-shafts can be clearly seen rising through the whole building. The atria work in a similar way, providing both light to the heart of the structure and an exhaust system through which warm air can rise and is then expelled. This kind of energy efficiency is beginning to become an issue in bank buildings but when this building was conceived it was still a highly radical approach. With the possible exception of Foster's DG Bank in Frankfurt, no other recent building has incorporated such a comprehensive set of energy-efficient features to the extent that these come to govern the whole appearance of the building. Efficient environmental control tends still to come tacked on as a supplementary feature.

The remarkable architectural expression of the bank is determined partly by the sinewy plan, partly by the repetitive plan shapes of the individual elements, partly by the demands of the prefabrication of building parts and partly by

*ABOVE, BELOW and OPPOSITE: The **ING Bank**, Amsterdam*

functional and environmental needs. As the building consists of ten broadly similar tower structures, prefabrication of the concrete slabs in the structure became an economical proposition. The exterior is clad in hand-made brick which acts not only as a thermal stabiliser but humanises the scale and colour of what would otherwise be an imposing and austere mass. It also knits the building into the well-founded Modernist Dutch brick tradition. The influence of the Expressionistic Amsterdam School architects, Michel de Klerk and Johann van der Mey in particular, is very clear in the sculptural use of brick and the complex massing of powerful volumes. Just as these architects who pioneered new forms of living, social housing and communal activity were heavily influenced by their Theosophical backgrounds and beliefs, this new approach to bank building betrays the architectural influence of Rudolf Steiner and his buildings based on his Anthroposophical ideas. This influence is perhaps even more powerfully felt in the building's interior where the spaces and the structure show the aversion to right angles which was characteristic of Steiner's work.

The interior spaces are free flowing, organic and open plan with each block being linked to its neighbours in a different way. The lower floors sprout out from the more rigorous and solid interlinking towers and are characterised by a freer plan, expansive glazing and double-height lobby and circulation spaces. The internal finishes are mostly concrete and timber, in contrast to the heavier brickwork which greets the visitor outside, and the extensive natural light is a surprise after the seemingly massive walls. Stairs, columns, balconies and roofs come together in a series of angular, almost Cubist, spatial geometries which express the dynamic nature of the circulation spaces. The effect owes much to Hans Scharoun's organic expressiveness and to Rudolf Steiner's sculptural moulding of concrete to express structure, mood, function and the meta-morphosis of natural forms. Trees and vines

inhabit the bright, airy atria to help humanise the interiors as well as to purify the air and these plant forms seem to emphasise the organic genesis of the architecture. Where natural light is not adequate, glass-encased lamps are constructed like fruit around columns and junctions reinforcing the powerful organic metaphors.

Whereas a number of architects have recently employed organic forms in major new bank buildings (Gehry and van Egeraat are the most notable), Alberts and van Huut are among the few to apply the principles consistently through-out the architecture. Perhaps only Günther Domenig has succeeded in producing such a distinctive organic bank building, albeit at a different scale. Yet despite this new Expressionism, Alberts and van Huut's design never resorts to the whimsical or to the level of gimmick, it is one of the most serious and intelligent major buildings of the last half of the twentieth century. It is one of the few to address critical questions of environmental design, human scale and comfort evolving a new architectural expression which springs from function rather than aesthetic theory. Its impact may be felt more powerfully in the longer term than has been the case in the years directly following its completion.

ARQUITECTONICA (ARQ)

The change from sober Modernism to witty and exuberant Post-Modernism in the architecture of the major banks and corporations is perhaps more visibly attributable to Arquitectonica than to any other office. Arquitectonica was responsible for a triumvirate of spectacular and conspicuous bank designs in the 1980s: the Banco de Credito in Lima, Peru (1982-88), the Banque de Luxembourg, Luxembourg (1989-91), and the Bank of America in Beverly Hills, California (1988-91). These buildings did for bank architecture what avant-garde firms like Memphis and designers including Ettore Sottsass and Aldo Rossi did for furniture and design objects. They introduced a glamorous, sexy and light-hearted approach which embraced an extravagant use of colour and a sculptural Post-Modern playfulness. This was all tempered with thoughtfulness, wit and the introduction of archetypal forms drawn from the archives of Italian Rationalism into the dull corporate world of headquarters buildings. Considering this playful approach and the tragically poor efforts of their imitators, their original creations have lasted well and continue to heavily influence bank design.

Their first major bank, the Banco de Credito in Lima, was a fantastic cocktail of theatrical forms around a simple quadrangle plan which recalls the earliest banks and exchanges, although here it was apparently inspired by the Spanish colonial courtyard buildings of the Americas. The quadrangle encloses a number of Inca ruins and ancient stone formations while a gap is left in the perimeter to allow a ridge of the Andes mountain range to continue within its boundaries, thus the building becomes a kind of arena containing a microcosmic version of the land and its history. The architects see the outer skin of the building, which is clad in stripes of black marble interspersed

OPPOSITE and ABOVE: **Banco de Credito**, *Lima, 1982-88*

with blue glass, as reflecting the corporate image and the modern city. The sculptural qualities of the interior facing, a local pink granite with holes punched at irregular intervals for the openings reflects a more formal, relaxed setting. The architectural interest of the interior of the quadrangle is compounded by a series of sculptural 'fragments' which are embedded in the rigid orthogonal mass of the rectilinear building and relate to the ancient fragments embedded in the rock at the bank's heart. An axis is created at a skewed angle through the building by the jagged break in the continuity of the perimeter wall and is picked up again by the elliptical reception area which is visible throughout the building so aiding orientation. Off this theatrical space a long corridor provides physical as well as visual access to the other wings. The public facilities within the building (cafeteria, auditorium, banking-floor and so on) are defined by volumes which slide through the massive colonnade which surrounds the building, differentiating them from the closed access areas. The roof includes luxurious features like a running track and swimming pool connected to leisure facilities within the building and also houses a heliport and telecommunications centre.

The Banque de Luxembourg headquarters building presented a very different proposition, an urban building in the centre of Luxembourg's financial district. The building is expressed as a composition of three distinct elements. A pink stone-clad facade with holes punched into it in a regular grid pattern is cantilevered out over the street and picks up the building line of the neighbouring structures tying the building into its context. This element, which contains the bulk of the building's floorspace, sits into a blank and rather ominously black granite-clad block at the end of which the third component appears. This third part of the composition is a segment of an ellipse which juts out from the main part of the building at a skewed angle and bridges the other two components. Beneath this jutting fragment a plaza is created within which a series of terraces is recessed into the ground, making an urban performance space. Virtually fully glazed, this prow-like element is the most visible part of the building, which is situated at the termination of a

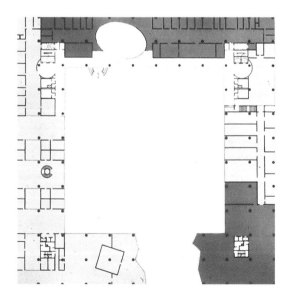

TOP and CENTRE: **Banco de Credito**, Lima
BELOW: Plan

boulevard. It is at its most dramatic at night, lit from within, when the dynamism and tension created by the clashing angles become fully apparent. In the building's sculptural interior, these same tensions become even more apparent. Curves, spirals and sharply angled corners construct an almost expressionistic sense of theatrical, or perhaps cinematic space, strong shadows and intense light creating a fascinating set of backdrops to the activities of the bank. The terracing beneath the glass tower begins to hint at the existence of an underground realm; the larger part of the building housing the main banking floor, trading rooms, vaults, computer centre and even a public auditorium, is in fact below ground.

ABOVE, CENTRE and BELOW: **Banque de Luxembourg**, *Luxembourg, 1989-91*

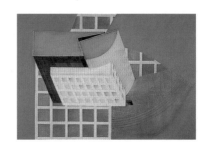

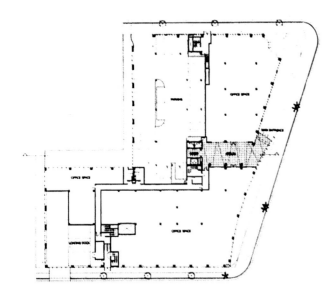

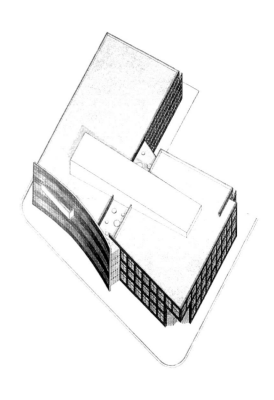

Bank of America, *California, 1988-91*

Paradoxically, the move from the quaint scenery of the conservative heartland of Europe to the epicentre of brash Post-Modernism, Los Angeles, resulted in an altogether more restrained and rational building for the Bank of America. The axonometric shows clearly that the building appears as two elements tending to peel away from each other and held together at the level of the roof by a kind of staple. This is the expression of the atrium rising above the roofline. At ground level the impression is of two distinct components, a sheer black screen tearing away from the rational gridded facade. The architects use the allusion of the plain black wall as a giant Cinerama screen set against a backdrop of the hills, none-too-subtle reference to the money of the Hollywood movie machine which finances the area. A corner of the office block with its rational glazing is stripped away to create an entrance to the building under the sharp canopy of the canti-levered second floor. Although the stapling form of the atrium at the top of the building is not visible from street level, the role of that element is fufilled by a sleek white balcony projecting from the black wall as a single white stripe. This device seems to anchor the wall into the bulk of the building beyond. Its slender, accentuated horizontal form also emphasises the tall, attenu-ated but irregular forms of the palm trees which frame the building. At the point at which the two walls peel away from one another, the passer-by gets a glimpse into the building through a full height window created at the gap.

Bank of America, *California*

BEHNISCH, BEHNISCH AND PARTNER

Built on the site of a part of Stuttgart's old fortifications, the service centre for the Landesgirokasse occupies a pivotal situation in the city between the old centre and the newer west end. The site is named the 'Bollwerk' (bulwark) and is elevated in a highly prominent position above the city. The intention of the architects was to exploit the high visibility of the site by creating a major new landmark to balance and resolve the rhythm set up by the city's other prominent buildings and thus to assist in the development of a specific character for the area. This sequence includes the castle, Stiftskirche, TV tower and the railway station. The architects have attempted to create a heart for this rather confusing urban site which has to address the problems of traffic and the local railway, a network of

overhead wires and cables, and a rather bland architectural setting. To avoid the building on this important site becoming a mere billboard for the wealth of the bank it was democratised by opening up its centre into a public courtyard. Although this is an administration and services centre, rather than a public bank or a lively exchange, it nevertheless builds on a tradition of the courtyard bank which stretches back to the Middle Ages, which is itself an architectural rationalisation of the market place.

The building is composed of two L-shaped blocks placed to form a square courtyard and leave a gap for access. One of the blocks is slightly skewed which helps to draw the public into the centre and breaks down the rigidity of this large structure which could otherwise become forbiddingly

OPPOSITE and BELOW: **Landesgirokasse**, *Stuttgart*

ABOVE and RIGHT: **Landesgirokasse**, *Stuttgart*

monolithic. Once inside the courtyard the barriers between internal and external, public and private spaces are comprehensively broken down using a series of architectural and spatial devices. The most striking of these is a large area of water, which reflects light back to other parts of the building, and a huge glass canopy. The interpenetration of these two elements reinforces a powerful spatial continuity between the lobby under its pitched glaze roof and the courtyard. The architectural expression strives to illustrate the semi-public nature of the autonomous lobby space which is used for public functions, receptions and exhibitions and which includes a café. The courtyard itself, the extension of the purely public realm, also becomes an exhibition space and is enlivened by a Frank Stella sculpture. The building also houses three cinemas, a restaurant and retail space.

Despite the objective to create a landmark building, the size is kept down to harmonise with its neighbours and is essentially a five-storey structure with the floors above the eaves level of its surroundings set back to reduce their impact. Only one element is allowed to break through this gentility and that is a long box housing an office wing and lounge which is dramatically cantilevered out over the street. Below this projecting block at street level, a slanted glazed wall begins to announce the themes of transparency and openness which are more fully explored in the interior of the complex.

OPPOSITE, ABOVE and LEFT: **Landesgirokasse**, *Stuttgart*

OPPOSITE, ABOVE and RIGHT: **Landesgirokasse**, *Stuttgart*

It is interesting to compare this scheme with the design which preceded it. The first, unbuilt scheme for the Landesgirokasse administration building was designed for a different site in Stuttgart. The design was also intended to fulfil the function of the urban landmark, albeit for a different part of the city (between mid- and west Stuttgart), but was designed to achieve this status in an altogether different fashion. The architects attempted to address the various urban situations inherent in the site while accommodating the huge amount of floorspace called for in the brief. To do this a relatively low elevation addresses the street side with a dramatic, glass-fronted lobby beneath it so that the mass of the building is raised on stilts. This fully visible lobby becomes a public space allowing both visual and physical access to the park and cemetery on the other side of the building. One element of the design then builds up in a series of terraces and floors into a stepped, irregular tower which avoids the problem of the monolithic block. The neighbouring block is kept lower. The design featured a remarkable lightness and penetrability despite its mass but after the project reached this advanced stage it was decided to hold another competition, the result of which is the building which can be seen here.

ABOVE, LEFT and OPPOSITE: **Landesgirokasse**, *Stuttgart*

ABOVE: **Banque Paribas**, *Paris, 1992-97; OPPOSITE: Site plan*

RICARDO BOFILL

Ricardo Bofill is known for a solid, monumental Classicism which was controversial in architectural circles, yet his large-scale housing schemes, ie Les Arcades du Lac in Saint Quentin-en-Yvelines (1974-80), were undoubtedly impressive, successful and popular with the public and instrumental in the formulation of the language of Post-Modern architecture. This background makes his design for the Paris headquarters of the Banque Paribas (1992-97) a rather surprising scheme. Built on the site of a historic Paris market the new bank building draws on the architecture of the nineteenth-century market hall for inspiration. Many of the advances in structural technology which inspired the architects of the Modern Movement were first made in market buildings

and, just as the British led the way in the design of railway stations which derived from similar roots, the French led the way in the field of market halls. As well as this architectural doff of the hat to market buildings, there is a close relationship between the architecture of banking, or more specifically exchange, and that of the covered market. Both building types were openly involved with commerce and trade and the architects of these buildings were often more concerned with function than with gesture, which was not the case in other fields. The great exchanges are money markets and the demands of the exchange and the market are not all that different, essentially a large open space, unencumbered by unnecessary accretions.

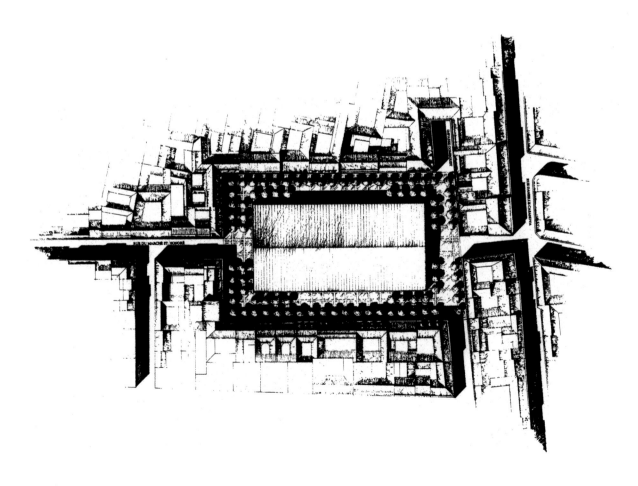

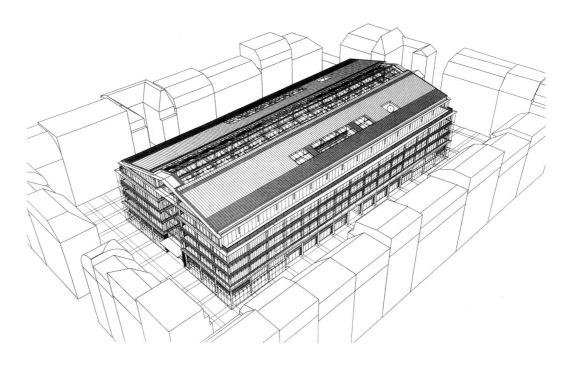

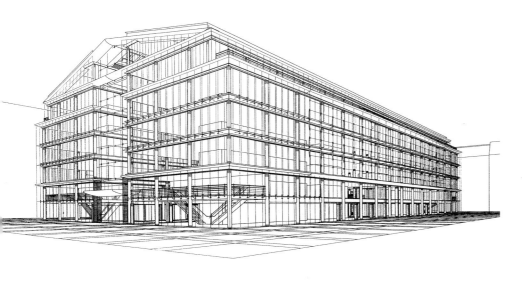

OPPOSITE and ABOVE: **Banque Paribas**, *Paris*

There is, however, a fundamental contradiction in the language of the open, public exchange and the private, closed and secure bank. It is these contradictions which make Bofill's scheme an unusual and enigmatic intervention into the urban fabric of Paris. The basic form and proportions of the building seem to be derived from a Greek temple. A pediment surmounts it and the main facade is sub-divided by a series of columns. Any similarities end there though; there is nothing Classical about these columns which are slender and run through a series of floors behind a glazed curtain-wall; the pediment too is merely an outline, glazed and transparent throughout. The centre of the building is hollowed out to create an internal street covered by a totally glazed roof which refers to the traditions both of the covered market hall and the more sophisticated version of the same principle, the glass-roofed shopping arcade. The site had previously been occupied by a monolithic multi-storey car park and this had blocked one of the city's historic axes – the visual connection between the Rivoli and the Opera.

*ABOVE, BELOW and OPPOSITE: **Banque Paribas**, Paris*

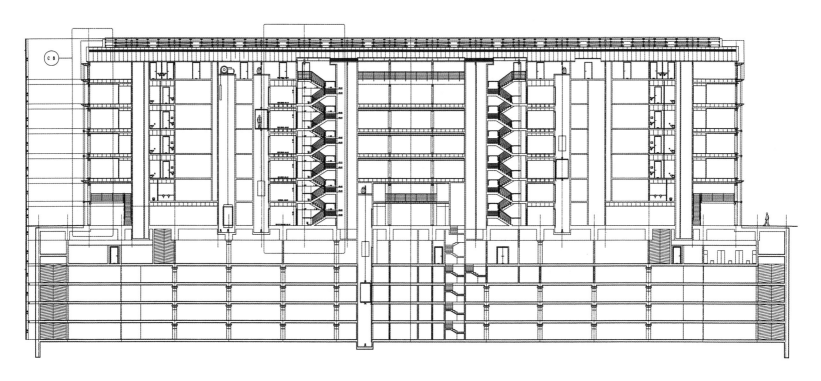

The central passage through the building is designed as a public space and a shopping arcade so that both the visual and the physical continuations of this important North–South axis are maintained. Like the temple which seems to have inspired the form of the building, its plan makes no concessions, other than the open spine, to the surrounding street plan. Rather, it is placed centrally on the site leaving generous public space all around it. This left-over space has been carefully landscaped and paved to create breathing space around what remains a large hulk of a building despite its transparency.

The building is completely transparent throughout, enclosed in a glazed curtain-wall through which the structure and the interior can be clearly seen, particularly at night. The simple I-beams at the edge of the floors display the simplicity of the structure behind the glass while the escalators in the bank's lobby and the bridges which link the two office blocks across the public corridor reveal the building's circulation systems and lay it bare to public scrutiny.

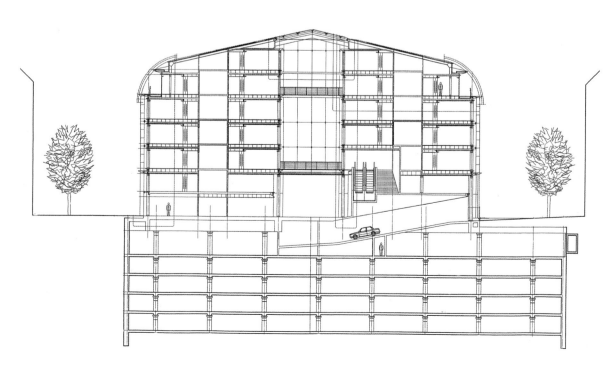

ABOVE and OPPOSITE: **State Bank**, *Fribourg, 1977-82*

MARIO BOTTA

The first of Mario Botta's four major bank buildings, the State Bank, Fribourg, Switzerland (1977-82), occupies a prominent corner site at a busy urban junction between two boulevards near a railway station. The architect indulged his passion for monumental Platonic solids with a huge curved half-cylinder which rises through the height of the building addressing the junction. This great drum becomes the pivot around which the building is organised. Its curve springs from a cubic volume to the fore of the site and behind this two rectangular wings pick up the building line of the streets which forms the V-shaped corner site. An opening, in the form of a loggia and terrace, in

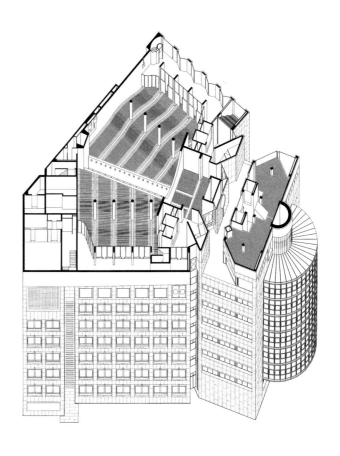

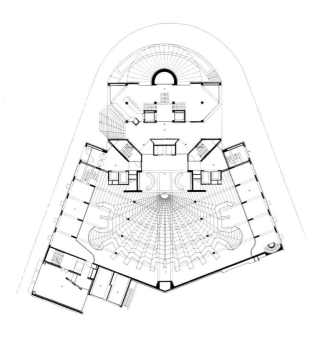

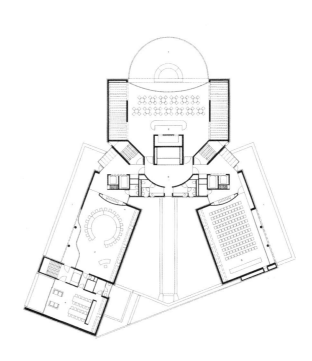

the cubic block behind the glazed drum implies that the cylinder continues within the structure and that only its front half is showing. In fact there is a concave curved, fully glazed wall above the cylinder which echoes the curve of the public front of the bank and behind this wall is situated the building's cafeteria with its own terrace on to the roof of the drum. The same shallow curve appears again as a repetitive motif throughout the building, not just in plan but also in elevation and as a modelling device. The main banking hall is dominated by a shallow arch of dramatically veined marble while the floor beneath is patterned with a series of circles of radiating lines of a similar material which culminate in a ring of counters, each also faced in the same marble. The ceiling above the banking hall is composed of an undulating surface of tubular elements at the centre of which a channel is cut in and opened up with glazing flooding the hall with light.

ABOVE and RIGHT: **State Bank**, *Fribourg*
OPPOSITE: **Banca del Gottardo**, *Lugano, 1982-88*

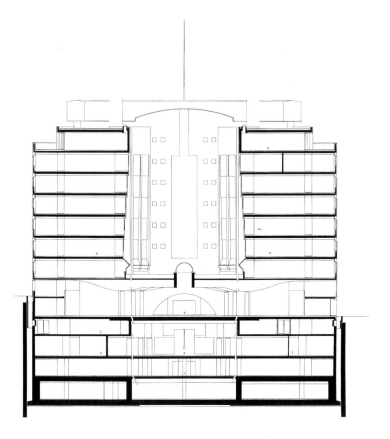

The headquarters building of the Banca del Gottardo in Lugano, Switzerland (1982-88), presents an altogether different conception of the place of the bank building in an urban setting. With this building, Botta attempts to break up the mass of the monolithic corporate building into a series of repetitive volumes which, although perceived as individual blocks, are manifestly parts of the same building. The four main elements are expressed as primitive blocks, cleft down the middle by a dark recess which begins to eat into their solidity in a series of toothed indents. Between these blocks are links which house circulation and service areas and these linking elements are recessed to leave the principal blocks distinct and separate. The gaps thus formed also create semi-enclosed courtyards which not only act as external atria and light-wells for the bank building but also as small public spaces, gestures of openness rather than exclusion towards the street. Planted with trees

and greenery, these small spaces also engage with the park on the opposite side of the road. The entrance is articulated by chamfered corners on the central split in the fabric of the block. A revolving door sets up a rigid central axis in the entrance block which is maintained throughout the interior, an axis emphasised by a join in the marble flooring which gives the curious appearance of a mirror placed at the centre of the space simply reflecting a single side.

The rear wall of the building is clearly the private side of the bank. Here too the mass of the building is broken up by a series of protruding blocks but there is none of the openness of the street elevation; between the uprights the length of the building is accentuated by the continuous bands of windows. The appearance is vaguely reminiscent of one of the visionary Futurist drawings of Antonio Sant'Elia, the monumental walls of the city of the future broken up by bastion-like service towers.

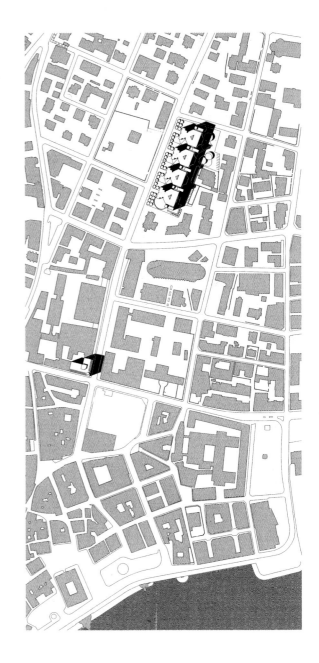

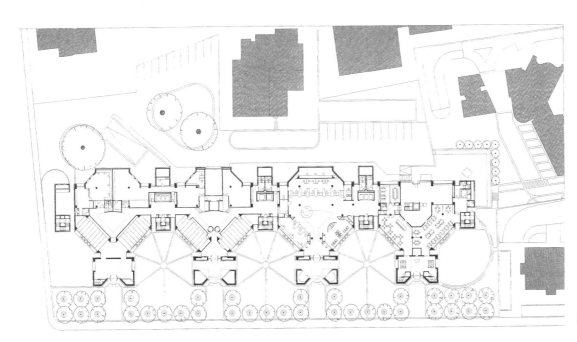

Banca del Gottardo, Lugano

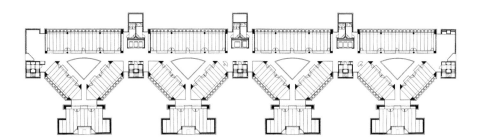

Banca del Gottardo, Lugano

ABOVE and OPPOSITE: **Union Bank of Switzerland**, *Basel, 1986-95*

The Union Bank of Switzerland Building in Basel, Switzerland (1986-95), is another huge urban structure in which the architect attempts to model the cityscape with a monumental presence placed at a busy and confusing junction. Botta has often spoken and written about the idea of buildings as faces within the city which people recognise as familiar characters within a townscape. This attempts to address a public alienated from their surroundings by the anonymous Modernist blocks which now populate cities, and return a sense of belonging and familiarity. The most significant of these architectural faces or masks are those belonging to the public institutions and places important to the cycle of public life – the church, theatre, station and the bank. There is something anthropomorphic about facade (the word after all derives from the same root as 'face') yet it is a rather indefinable quality. Perhaps the broad curve and the symmetry of the elevation assist in giving form to a kind of human recognition. A pair of stepped cut-outs creates the facial features and the building is capped off by a row of porthole openings which reveal the sky beyond. The large curve of the facade also allows the bank building to be separate and distinct from a neighbouring nineteenth-century villa and to act as a fulcrum between the angles of buildings on the two sides of the bank. The impression of the building from the street is of a huge cylinder and it is rather a surprise to find that it is only a curved section. The orange-segment shape of the building becomes evident within the bank with views up into the central light-well and the great curved, open office areas of the upper floors.

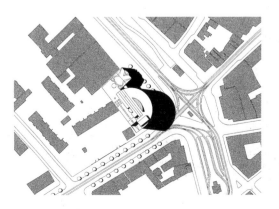

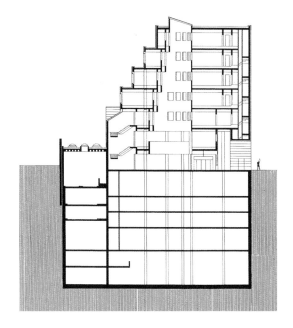

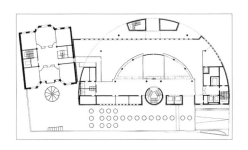

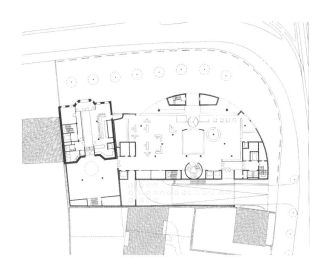

Union Bank of Switzerland, *Basel*

Botta's building for the Banque Bruxelles Lambert, Geneva, Switzerland (1987-96), is a more restrained and humble structure which sits in a tight urban site, its dimensions in almost all directions were laid out in the competition brief and the master-plan for this quarter of the city. The narrower elevation of the building facing the main road and public space opposite is split into two towers by a central fissure. Botta's notion of the building as mask again becomes apparent here as an arcade at street level and two square openings higher up the elevation seem to re-present a face with the central split approximating a nose. The entrance, however, is not from this most prominent facade but from the centre of the longer elevation to the side. Here too a deep cleft

Banque Bruxelles Lambert,
Geneva, 1987-96

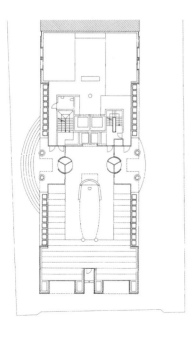

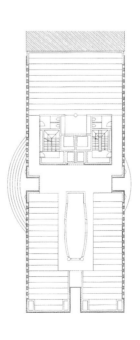

in the fabric of the elevation signifies the point at which the heavy masonry wall parts to create an opening. In contrast to Botta's other bank buildings, the rigidly symmetrical elevation of the Bank Bruxelles Lambert opens to an asymmetrical interior. On one side of the lobby, which runs right through the width of the narrow building, is placed the vertical circulation while on the other side an atrium with gently curving walls runs up through the whole height of the interior culminating in a glass vault which illuminates the building below.

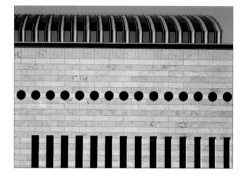

Banque Bruxelles Lambert

ODILE DECQ AND BENOÎT CORNETTE

It seems that many European banks and large financial institutions, when they begin to think about commissioning major new buildings, display a great fondness for the works of architects who are associated with High-Tech. Foster's Hong Kong and Shanghai Bank and Commerzbank, in Frankfurt, or Richard Rogers' Lloyds Insurance Building in London, or to an extent, John McAslan's Yapi Kredi Bank in Turkey (although this latter is a blend of other approaches as well) seem to justify the assumption. Possibly this relates to a notion which is held fondly by these institutions of the bank as an efficient, High-Tech, money-making machine. It is largely British architects who are associated with this particular style, even if it is not always British clients who commission these works. In fact it was the French who commissioned Rogers' Centre Beaubourg in Paris, perhaps defining the High-Tech architecture

*OPPOSITE and ABOVE: **Banque Populaire de l'Ouest et d'Armorique**, Rennes, 1988-90*

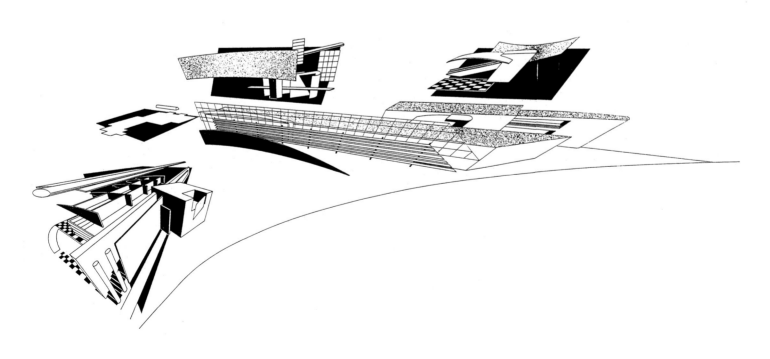

at a time when it was making little progress in Britain. This building represented the beginning of a curious love/hate relationship with High-Tech architecture between the British and the French. Certainly much of the original inspiration for High-Tech had come from France. Jean Prouvé and Pierre Chareau are heralded as early prophets, the Modernist delight in construction as expression found fruition in the work of these pioneers. A handful of French architects have themselves recently reinterpreted and blended these High-Tech influences. Among these new interpreters were Odile Decq and Benoît Cornette. Cornette was involved in a fatal accident in 1998 although Odile Decq is continuing the experimentation.

One of Decq and Cornette's fullest explorations of the language of High-Tech is the Banque Populaire de l'Ouest et d'Armorique near Rennes in France (1988-90). The complex consists of three separate buildings: an existing computer centre and the new buildings by Decq and Cornette, an office building and a social centre for the bank staff. The office building is characterised by an extremely long south-facing glazed wall, designed in conjunction with engineer Peter Rice. Behind this a concave mirrored aluminium wall reflects the complex construction of the

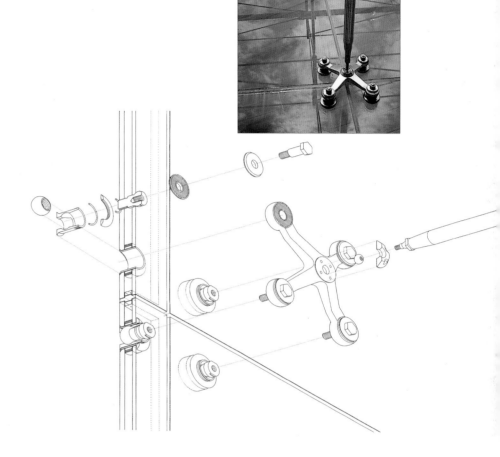

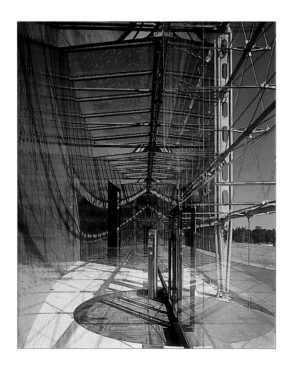

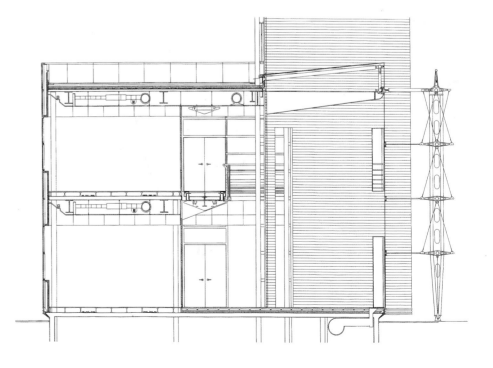

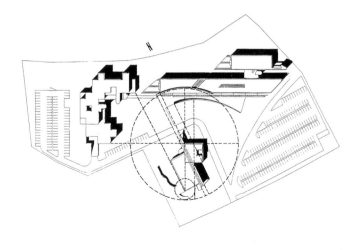

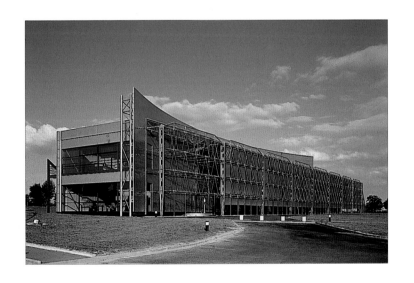

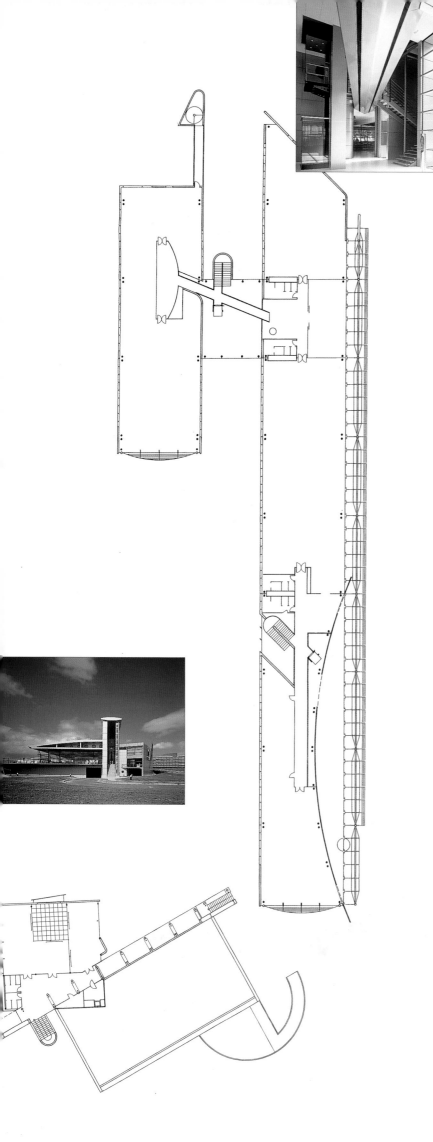

glazed wall's framing, which is all external leaving the glass wall itself to stand unencumbered, and the great expanse of sky above. The main entrance is through a breach in this concave wall. A series of panels of blinds behind the glazing can be lowered to prevent excessive solar gain. Illuminated at night, the building presents a facade of pure light; it would be hard to imagine a more effective billboard. The main block tails off beyond the glazed wall and tapers into a prow, an image which is reinforced by the inclusion of three port-hole windows. Behind this block is a smaller, plainer building which terminates in a sculptural external stair. This consists of a metal cage within which a bright blue spiral stair rises, the elegant curving handrails of the structure again alluding to a maritime theme.

The other block is articulated in a smoother, more clinical manner. Aluminium cladding throughout evokes a machine-like precision. This part of the building is composed of two blocks; one with a square plan which is aligned with the administration block and which then crashes into the corner of a larger block so that tension is created in the skewed angle of the junction. The smaller, square building houses a meeting room and offices while the larger block which meets it at one corner houses an expansive staff restaurant. Throughout this part of the building the stripped industrial, structural aesthetic proliferates. Columns and trusses are all left in exposed steel, their perforated forms allowing light to penetrate even the structural elements, lending a great lightness to all parts of a building which is already extensively glazed. The constantly changing northern French light and the spindly structural elements throw fascinating shadows across all the surfaces of the building which are continuously in flux so that the structures are enlivened by movement and shade.

GÜNTHER DOMENIG

Günther Domenig's Z-Bank in Vienna is undoubtedly the most unorthodox building featured in this book and it is one of only a few which date back to before the 1980s. Although I have attempted to keep this book broadly within the frame of the last decade or so I have made a few exceptions with the inclusion of earlier buildings which I feel were pivotal in the development of new ideas about bank architecture. Among these key buildings I have included Kisho Kurokawa's Fukuoka Bank (1971-75) and Norman Foster's Hongkong and Shanghai Bank (1979-86), the designs of both of which date back to the 1970s. The design of the Z-Bank (1975-79) falls exactly between these two other buildings and it is useful to see them together to get an idea of historical context. The 1960s had seen an outburst of fantastic architectures inspired as much by science-fiction and by predictions of an uncertain global and environmental future as by genuine technological and design innovations. These included Metabolism in Japan within which Kurokawa was a leading figure; the emergence of a kind of agit-prop, comic-book High-Tech architecture in England which Foster was to begin to realise in built form along with Richard Rogers; and the resurgence of an organic architecture in Central Europe principally in Germany, Austria and Hungary. Although the genesis of these movements was rooted in the counter-culture of the 1960s they were all to reach fruition a decade later. Of this group of three buildings, Domenig's was the most radical and remains the most startling.

Domenig was instrumental in the development of what has become known as the Graz School.

Z-Bank, Vienna, 1975-79

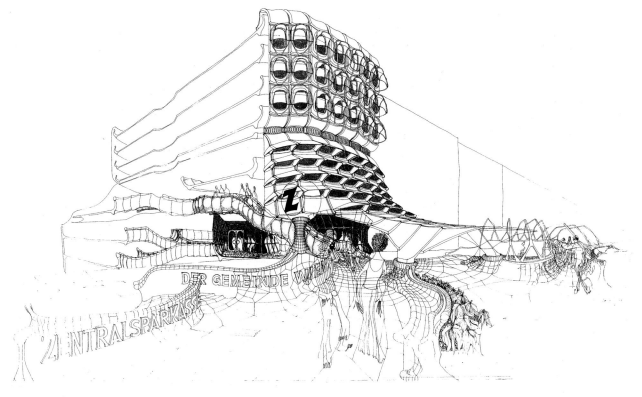

Although not a formal grouping, a handful of Graz architects developed an organic, highly individualistic approach which drew on early Expressionist experiments, science-fiction visionaries and the work of Rudolf Steiner as well as on the organic branch of Modernism for inspiration. It became defined in contrast to the Viennese establishment which was seen as rigid, formal and weighed down by the dogma of its illustrious Modernist forebears, Wagner and Loos. Thus it is interesting to look at Domenig's building as a reaction to the other Viennese bank featured here, Wagner's own Postal Savings Bank. Wagner represents the model of rationalism and of respect for context. Domenig's building three quarters of a century later can be seen as a rebellion against the constraints of that rational world. The building's bulging metal-clad facade crumples up at the centre to create an entrance on an otherwise

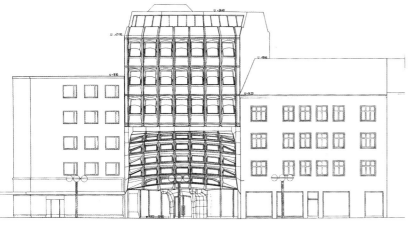

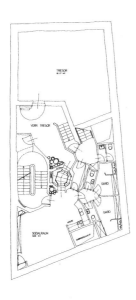

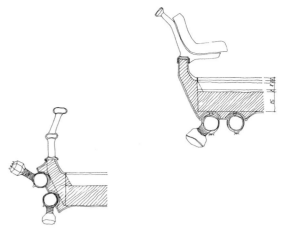

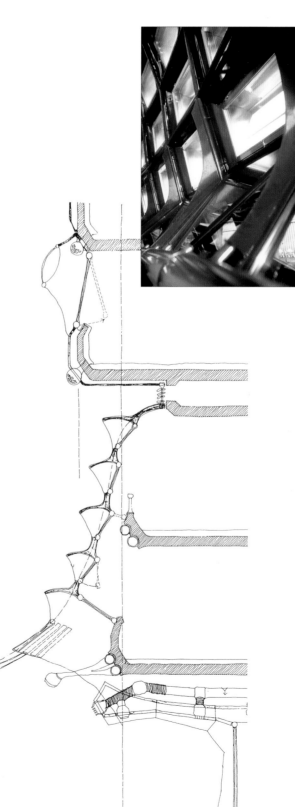

unremarkable Vienna shopping street, the Favoriten. The crumpled metal forms a canopy under which a steel and glass framework, a jagged neon tongue, lumpy concrete and deformed columns lead into the heart of the building. The architect's sketches give an idea of the organic tangle of structure and services which inhabits the building's interior. The feel is of being inside a great organism, a building which is living and breathing. There is something reminiscent of the interior landscapes of the science-fiction films *Fantastic Voyage* (1966), in which a team of doctors is shrunken and injected into a human body, and *Brazil* (1985) in which a nightmare future world lives in fear of the jumbled mass of ducts and services which lurk behind its walls and which could (and do) fail at any time. Like director Terry Gilliam's vision of the future in *Brazil*, the Z-Bank presents a world which is tragi-comic, serious architecture with touches of humour and humanity. The architect's hand is present in a more than metaphorical sense: the interior is dominated by a massive sculpture of the architect's own right hand which seems to be actively sculpting the distorted forms of the interior. A ramshackle spaghetti of ducts and pipes, trusses and lighting tubes lurks overhead while in the space itself, the absence of the architectural tyranny of the right angle is noticeable. This

powerfully recalls the work of Rudolf Steiner who avoided squares and right angles as oppressive and inhuman geometries. The organic, sculptural, concrete frame of the building which can be seen throughout, but is particularly noticeable in the building's stairs, also shows a great debt to Steiner, in particular the second Goetheanum at Dornach (1924-28).

A facade of the same elemental, metal-clad composition addresses the rear of the site but whereas on the front of the building the elevation crumples into a canopy like a crashed car body, at the rear it sprouts a dramatic glass roof consisting of large triangular panes in an organically shaped frame which allows light into the lower floors. This remarkable building presaged later developments in organic architecture and what would later be loosely termed Deconstruction. There is a close relationship with the organic brickwork in the basement of Kisho Kurokawa's Fukuoka Bank, completed in the same year that the Z-Bank was designed, and with the High-Tech constructional

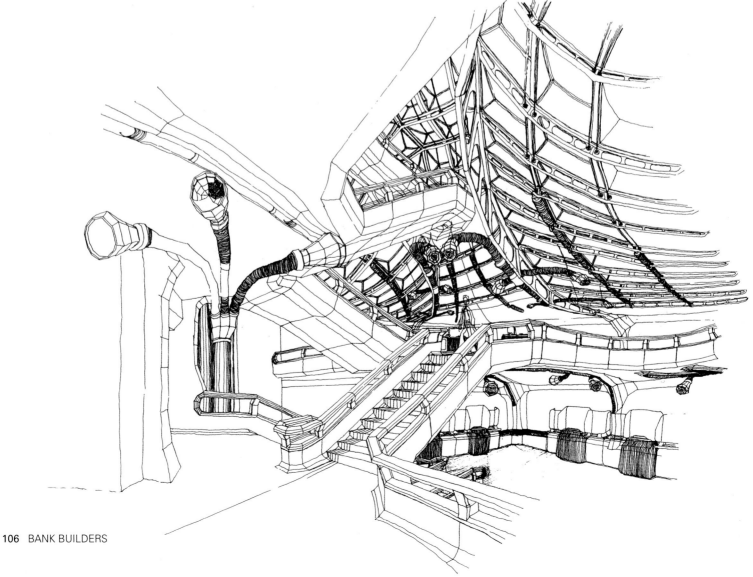

elements of Foster's Hongkong and Shanghai Bank, designed in the year the Z-Bank was completed. However, Domenig perverts and distorts the tectonic features which Foster revels in and deliberately allows to dominate the building. In this way we can see parallels here not only with the visionary set design for Terry Gilliam's *Brazil* but also with the later designs of Lebbeus Woods which see organic/machine elements breaking through the structure in a nightmare vision akin more to HR Giger's *Alien* designs than to Terry Gilliam. The organic element which intrudes the roofspace in Erick van Egeraat's ING Bank in Budapest and the dramatic forms of Behnisch, Behnisch and Partner's Landesgirokasse Bank in Stuttgart also illustrate how this kind of thinking has created a demand for avant-garde sculptural and Expressionistic architecture within the notoriously conservative world of banking. The Z-Bank represents a pivotal landmark in individualistic and Expressionist bank design and the shock waves it sent through architecture are still being felt.

ERICK VAN EGERAAT

Built in two phases, the Hungarian office of the ING Bank (1992-97) represents one of the finest and most thoughtful of the recent architectural interventions into the dense urban fabric of Budapest. The first phase involved the conversion of an existing building on the city's principal Boulevard, Andrássy út, into modern bank and office accommodation. To achieve this the building's courtyard was turned into an internal atrium; the original windows, doors and walkways were retained and restored so that the space at the heart of the building remains a circulation area and provides the dense urban block with a single, impressive open space. This also has the effect of maintaining the essence of the Central European courtyard building type which gives the inner city its character. Standing in the converted courtyard the eye is drawn skywards by a striking form at roof level. An amorphous lump lurks above the atrium, the contrast between the amoeba-like form of this element and the heavy Classicism of the old building is highly effective and makes manifest the difference between existing and new elements. The roof-level blob houses the conference room and refocuses attention on the heart of the building. Referred to by the architects as 'the whale', the single organic element is never visible in its entirety either inside or outside the building yet its presence is felt from all parts of the bank. Fragments which can be glimpsed throughout the building add to its enigmatic presence.

The newly restored sculptural elements and details on the main elevation, now fully illuminated, exert a powerful presence on the boulevard and contrast strikingly with the sheer Modernism glimpsed within the building. The bank accommodation penetrates the whole urban block and the architecture which emerges in the smaller, narrower backstreet behind is utterly different to the monumental restored facade at the front. The rear elevation is expressed as a sheer wall of glass which leans outwards at an angle of six degrees. Whereas the boulevard on which the main elevation sits is in good order, a well-maintained shopping street, the facades of the buildings surrounding the bank at the rear are decaying, their plaster peeling and the Classical mouldings encrusted with years of dirt. The new facade gleams in the light yet reflects the decay of its surroundings. It seems an ironic take on the Post-Modern mirror glass phenomenon, the

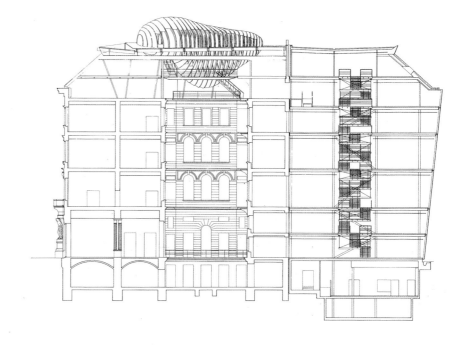

OPPOSITE and RIGHT: **ING Bank**, *Budapest, 1992-97*

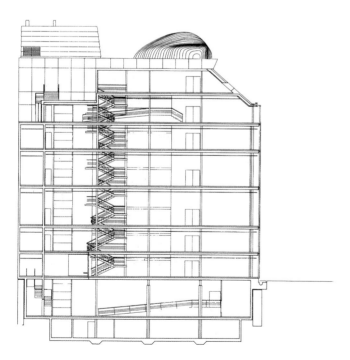

building deliberately drags itself down to the level of its neighbours not reflecting the sky but the earthy colours and crumbling walls of its urban context. The reflections in the facade seem to pull the neighbouring buildings closer like some powerful architectural magnet so that, despite the difference in the architectures, this is a building which reacts to its neighbours while powerfully exerting its own presence.

The building turns the corner once more and, as was required by local planning regulations, adopts the scale and rhythm of its neighbours with a clever flourish. The effect of solid wall and window opening is created using clear glass and glass which has been silk-screen printed, using computer-generated pixels, in imitation of the graining patterns of stone. The facade is completely glazed and flush throughout yet it appears as an

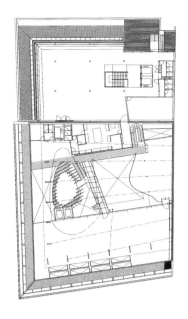

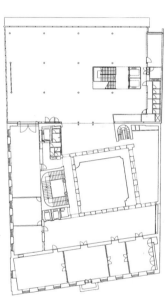

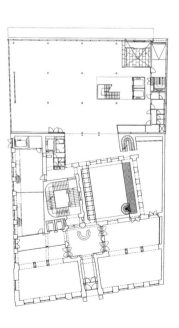

understated traditional elevation which in colour and rhythm blends in subtly with its surroundings. From within the effect is similar to what would have been achieved using wafer-thin sheets of stone; a translucent surface in which the grain shows through in the light. The effect is intriguingly visible on close inspection of the glass and it has an almost disturbing surrealistic quality to it. The completely glazed facade allows light to penetrate even the deepest parts of the building. At night the effects of illumination are remarkable; while the stone effect becomes opaque and light is only admitted through the clear openings, the slanted facade reveals a sectional view of the building. It is worth comparing the transparent democracy of this building with both Wagner's Postal Savings Bank and the simple punched openings and glazed central hall of Ödön Lechner's nearby Postal Savings Bank. Almost a century later, van Egeraat has taken the advances made by these pioneers to a fine-tuned conclusion and designed a humane and intelligently urban solution to bank architecture which nevertheless manages to embrace the advances of new materials and technologies to create modern, forward-looking and supremely elegant forms.

Central Bank of Malta, *Valletta, 1993*

RICHARD ENGLAND

One of the pivotal notions that architects have always had to address in the design of a banking institution is that of security; not merely of actual security but of visual security, the appearance of impenetrability. Sir John Soane's expressively massive, blind Classical wall which contains the Bank of England is perhaps the supreme example of the genre but its genesis can be easily traced back to the oversized rustication of the Florentine *palazzi* commissioned by the pioneering dynasties of modern international banking. Looked at from this angle, Richard England's Central Bank of Malta in Valletta, Malta (1993), begins with a distinct advantage. The head start is that the new bank is barricaded behind the massive walls of a section of the city's sixteenth-century fortifications. The building was designed in such a way that it would slot into the bastion without damaging the original walls and without impinging on their appearance or profile when seen from below.

The bank's three storeys are accommodated within the bastion and below the level of the battlements and are fully visible only from above. The building is organised around a central atrium which allows light to penetrate the deep floors which would otherwise be deprived of light and air as they are bounded by the huge walls of the bastions. It is entered via a drum-shaped portico

structure which sets up the central axis of the building that sits squarely and symmetrically within the fortifications. The public areas of the bank and the banking hall itself are to the front of the building and the administration spaces are located towards the rear section of the bank. A corridor is maintained around the perimeter of the building adjacent to the existing bastion walls which provides not only fire escape routes but also a differentiation between the new and the old structures. The bank's walls are of a local stone, whose colour does not interfere with that of the stones of the fortifications, yet their smooth ashlar surfaces are evidently not part of the old structure. The bank is bounded by an enclosed garden incorporating sculptures by the architect and on the other side by the original chapel to the site.

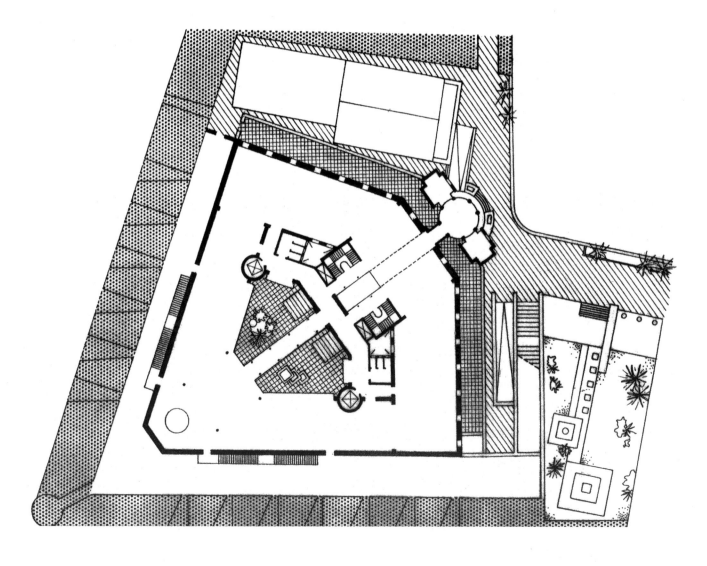

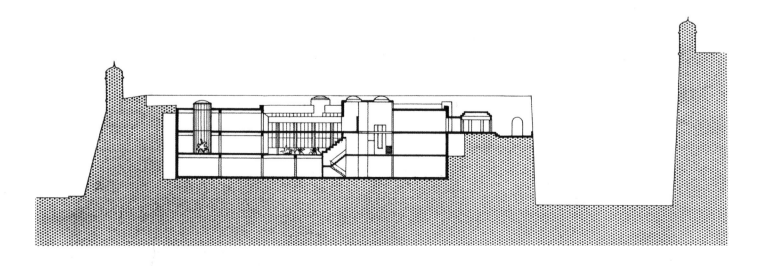

EPR

The enduring legacy of Expressionist architecture is the image of the spiky glass building, a development of the idea of the crystal mountain, a motif which dominated the short-lived but influential creative outburst of the movement. The image represented the world mountain, a mystical view of the cosmos as a brilliantly sparkling, reinvigorated landscape. These notions were inextricably linked not only with mysticism but with socialism and revolution. Mies van der Rohe came closest to realising these glass fantasies in his skyscraper designs of the 1920s and then developed his ideas into the glass box which was subsequently adopted by the corporate world and became the model of the capitalist establishment. It is fascinating then to see a revival of the original, angular image of the early Expressionist designs just outside the traditional boundaries of London's financial district.

EPR's new building for ABN AMRO (1996-99) has to cope with an oddly shaped site and a curious and sensitive setting with the monumental Broadgate office and retail development on one side of the road, the historic Spitalfields area behind it and the close proximity of Charles Harrison Townsend's pioneering Bishopsgate Institute (1894), one of the seminal buildings in the development of Arts and Crafts and Art Nouveau architecture. The new bank building expresses the angular shape of the sharply pointed corner site with an almost jagged glass structure which does not compete with the mass and solidity of any of these dominant buildings. Rather, there is a delicate transparency and fineness of construction which create a foil for them and a crystalline termination to the growing financial district. The building presents a series of facades, each tailored to its surroundings from the ten-storey elevation to the main road to three storeys to the smaller-scale Spitalfields Market area at the back of the site. The structure is

ABN AMRO, London, 1996-99

expressed on the exterior of the building in a series of tubular columns which look as if they were pipes appearing at regular intervals. These allow the structure to be taken outside the building leaving the maximum amount of unencumbered floorspace within and yet their slender simplicity does not interfere with the views through the windows.

The bank is entered through a chamfered corner on the main road which leads to an atrium rising through three storeys within which the reception area, scenic lifts and escalators are housed. Beyond this the building is split into two distinct parts. The first part occupies the whole of the site and rises through to the second-floor level housing the kind of deep uninterrupted floorspace required for dealing rooms, each of these opens on to the entrance atrium. The upper floors wrap around another atrium (beginning at the third floor level) at the centre of the building in a kind of delta shape and within these floors is housed the office accommodation. The elevations are expressed in metal and glass and culminate in a tall mast rising into the sky at the corner of the building which draws the eye upwards to the acutely angled corner. This presents the most memorable, expressionistic view of the building, a kind of cosmic glass mountain to the delicate tree of life designs which appear on Townsend's neighbouring Bishopsgate Institute; the bank as expression of the world of finance.

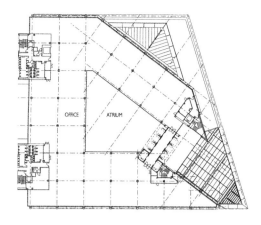

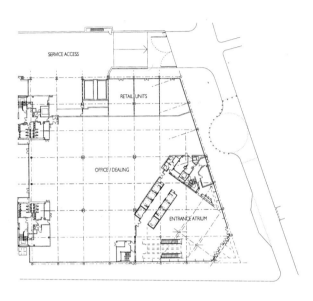

EPR's Old Broad Street development, occupied by the Halifax and Bankers' Trust, is a building almost the diametric opposite of the ABN AMRO headquarters. Solid and stoneclad on the outside, there is none of the radical jaggedness of Bishopsgate, but then this is a building nearer the heart of the conservative City of London. Within the building, however, an off-centre atrium reveals a High-Tech core; a vibrant space at the heart of the building which serves to provide light and orientation within the deep floor plates but also accommodates the building's circulation system with a series of galleries and stairs and banks of lifts opening out from it. The eye is drawn up the atrium towards the curving elements of the roof structure and beyond to the sky above.

*OPPOSITE: **Old Broad Street Development**, Halifax and Bankers' Trust*
BELOW: Old Broad Street
ABOVE: Old Broad Street atrium roof; section and elevation

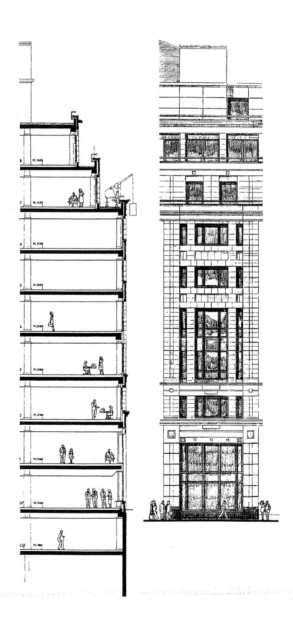

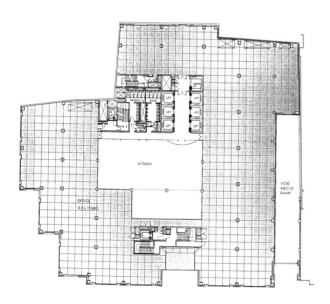

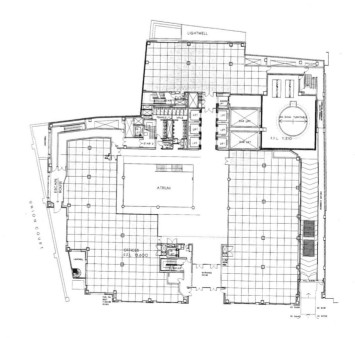

Old Broad Street

FOSTER ASSOCIATES

The Hongkong and Shanghai Bank headquarters (1979-86) in Hong Kong and the Commerzbank headquarters in Frankfurt (1994-97) are without doubt two of the most influential bank buildings of the second half of the twentieth century. The former in particular was to define a particular moment in the story of banking (the tremendous surge of confidence in the wake of international deregulation) perhaps more eloquently than any other building. Both buildings are eloquent expressions of optimism in the banking sector (the boom of the 1980s and the creation of a new currency and a new financial capital in Europe) and the structures also mark pivotal moments in the development of the cities over which they cast their long shadows. The Hongkong and Shanghai Bank succeeded an earlier headquarters building which had become synonymous with money in Hong Kong to the extent that, as one of the two money-issuing banks on the island, its image was featured on the one hundred dollar note. Foster's bank therefore had to create a new icon for the island.

The building which Foster created for the Hongkong and Shanghai Bank has become per-haps the single most successful example of bill-board bank architecture. An individualistic, instantly recognisable structure it has become, like its predecessor, synonymous with the power and influence of capital on this tiny island, a power so profound that even the Communists have surrendered to it and left Hong Kong's rampantly successful markets alone. The building is a curious blend of power and delicacy, of muscular High-Tech and pure transparency. The massive structural system is placed on the outside like an exoskeleton, graphically illustrating the forces and the weight of the building yet it allows the central section to be pure open space, glazed and continuous with the notion of the wall as

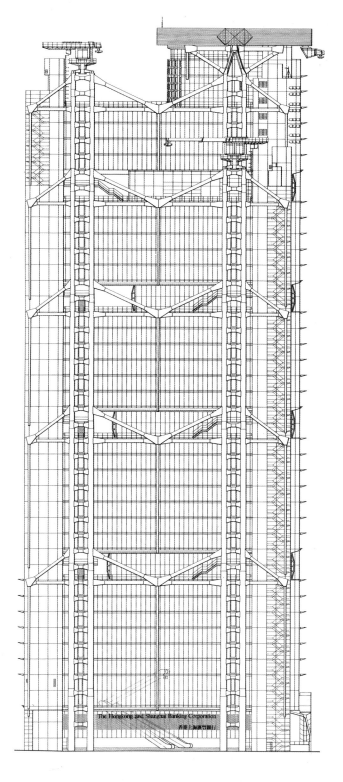

Hongkong and Shanghai Bank, *Hong Kong, 1979-86*

barrier disappearing altogether. This idea of spatial continuity between outside and in which permeates all levels of the building is most clearly visible at ground level where a public circulation space is created beneath the building. This gesture is virtually unprecedented in a city where public space is almost unbearably scarce. Above this open public space the great bowed glass belly of the building separates the air-conditioned environment of the interior from the open air below and allows views up into the structure. Escalators convey the visitor up into the heart of the building and announce the circulation dynamic of the rest of the building. Rather than huge banks of lifts serving every floor, high-speed lifts serve only the double-height reception floors and the building user takes escalators up or down from there to the desired floor. The result is a cascade of escalators flowing at skewed angles (the placing and angles of some are determined by *feng shui*) through the building and creating a sense of movement throughout the interior.

The elevations express as much of the building's dynamics as do the interiors as it is here that the structure comes into view; colossal masts off which the building's floors are hung like loads from a tower crane. The scale of the structure is pure science fiction, recalling the fantastic visions of gargantuan space stations but also the more familiar language of the oil platform; a huge structure which seems to be drilling for money on the coast of Hong Kong. But as well as the High-Tech language there are also allusions to Asian tectonic languages, both archaic and recent. Foster cites the pagoda as an inspiration for the structural form of the elevations, the tiered roofs being compared to the great trusses. By implication the symbolic function of the pagoda as a world-model (the representation of the multiple layers of heaven and earth) and as an image of the world mountain, gives validity to the notions of solidity and stability which are crucial to the image of a bank but also sets the building up as a bridge between the earth and the heavens. In a more direct way the building also recalls the modular, High-Tech visions of the Japanese Metabolists, who were themselves influenced by British Pop architecture – the closing of a neat circle.

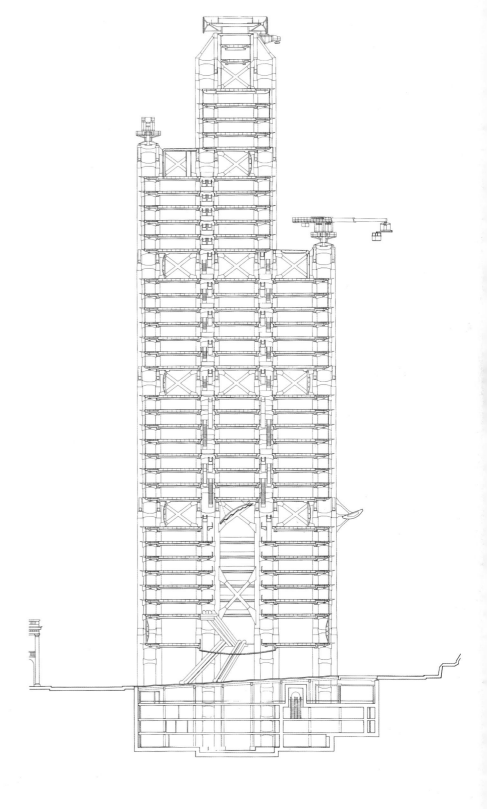

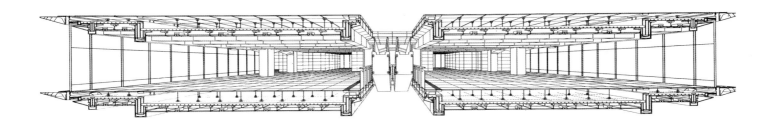

Section through a typical floor

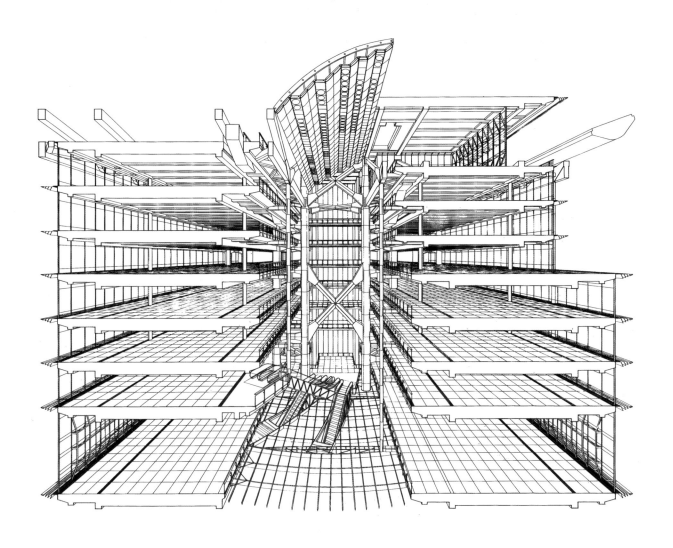

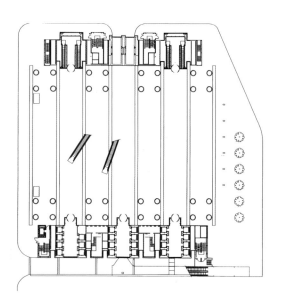

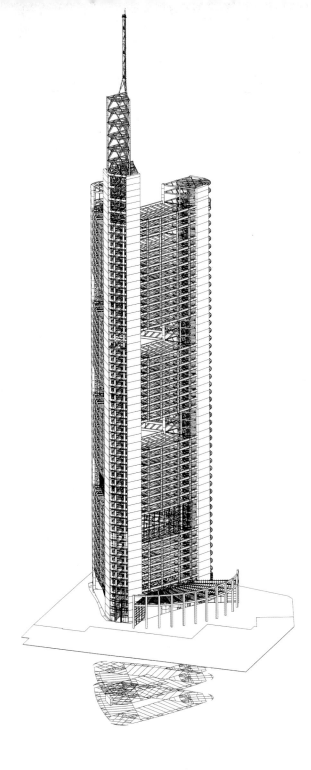

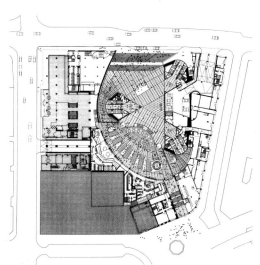

Commerzbank, Frankfurt, 1994-97

The next pivotal bank building to be realised by Foster and Partners was the Commerzbank in Frankfurt. The German financial capital has fought hard to assert itself as the new financial capital of a united Europe. London has traditionally been the banking centre of Europe and Frankfurt has struggled to usurp London's dominance of the international money markets. A major component of the effort to create a credible new financial capital for Europe in competition with London has been the construction of new bank buildings on a huge scale. However, even here, Frankfurt finds itself almost eclipsed by Berlin, where a tremendous surge is taking place in bank building as a result of the city becoming the new German capital and banks relocating to prestigious sites in the city centre. The two most dramatic structures which have begun to define the new character of Frankfurt, which already an incredible wealth of modern arts buildings, are two massive banks: Foster's Commerzbank and KPF's towering DG Bank. The brief for the Commerzbank, the tallest building in Europe at the time of its completion, bizarrely called for an eco-friendly skyscraper, a seeming contradiction in terms. As a building type the skyscraper is notoriously expensive and wasteful of energy both in the construction and running costs. There are some ingenious innovations in the relatively simple plan of the Commerzbank which make this a green building in more ways than that for which the phrase is conventionally used. A series of gardens rises up the building in a spiralling pattern providing ventilation and greenery throughout. This is achieved within a plan which has had its edges and corners chamfered in smooth curves. Within this shape a triangular core is created and this becomes an atrium which rises up through the entire height of the building. Around this central core three distinct floor zones are created. These are separated from each other by the service cores which occur at the corners on all floors. On any floor, two of these floor zones house office space while the third is given over to a garden. Each garden rises up through four storeys and is situated in a twisting rhythm moving around the building as it ascends. This pattern of gardens amplifies the positive effects of the stack

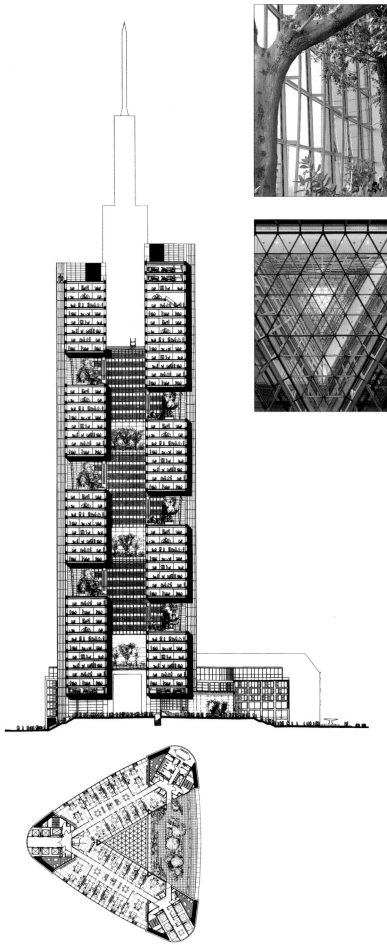

system produced by the use of the central atrium and creates natural ventilation throughout the building to the extent that mechanical ventilation is provided only as back up. The office floor zones are split by a central spine corridor so that, in every instance, one set of offices will have views out away from the building while the other will have an aspect on to the central atrium, the garden across from it and beyond to the world outside. Lifts and stairs are situated in the service cores at the corners which also hold the building up. They rise uninterrupted through the height of the building where floors appear as protruding bays between the full-height glazing sections of the periodic winter gardens. The points of the corners are glazed and the structural role is undertaken by the massive walls which create the sides of these corners. This gives the tower an appearance of lightness and sleekness as if it were aerodynamically, rather than merely structurally engineered; perhaps a reference to Foster's keen admiration for the economy and pure functionalism of the design of aeroplanes. Foster and Partner's most recent excursion into bank building has been with the new offices for Citibank in London's Canary Wharf (1997-99). Much more strikingly simple than the two previous buildings the design recalls the crystalline idealism of the early Modernists and it is undoubtedly one of the most elegant Modernist blocks in London of recent years and may be joined by another building currently being proposed at the Baltic Exchange site in London.

*ABOVE: **Commerzbank**: Section and plan*
*OPPOSITE: **Citibank**, Canary Wharf, London, 1999*

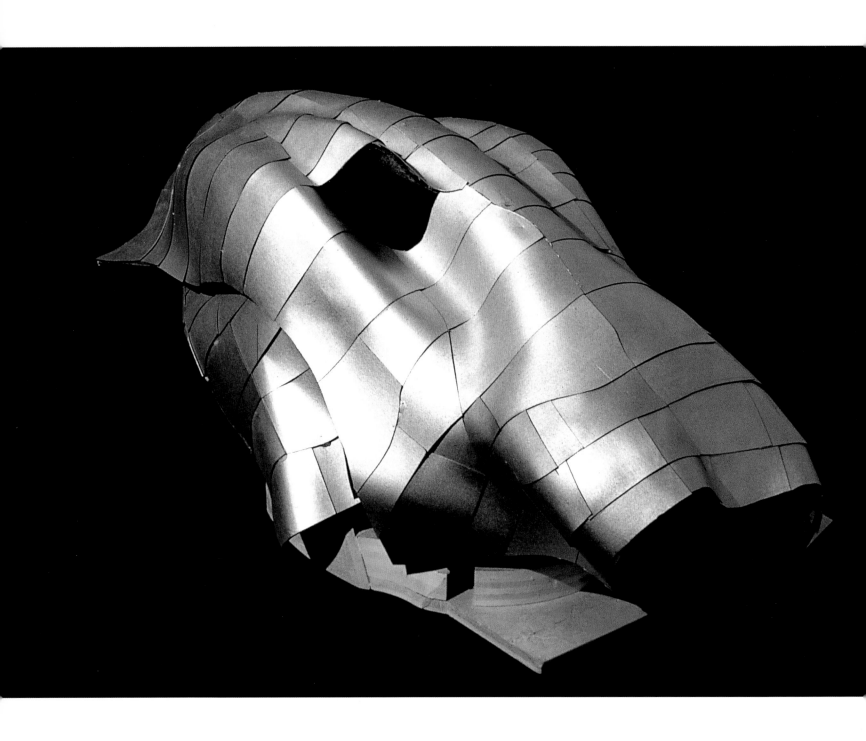

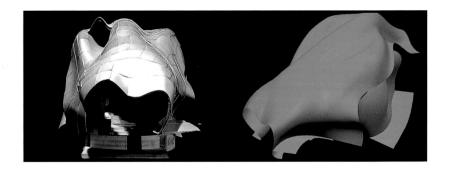

FRANK O GEHRY

The context for Gehry's new DG Bank is the Brandenburg Gate. Situated on the Pariser Platz, the gate has become the symbol of Berlin and for years it was the most poignant sign of the divided city; a triumphal arch stripped of victory. Built in the year of the outbreak of the French Revolution (1789), it was damaged in the Second World War and repaired the year of the outbreak of the Hungarian Revolution (1956) which saw the first concerted effort by an Eastern Bloc country to overthrow the yoke of Soviet domination. What armed struggle could not do, the lure of capital and freedom eventually achieved in a peaceful fashion in both Germany and Hungary. One modern bank building in Hungary has been featured in this book and it is interesting and instructive to compare that building to Gehry's new creation. The Hungarian building is Erick van Egeraat's ING Bank in downtown Budapest. Initially the two schemes seem very different; the Budapest ING Bank is a conversion of an existing apartment block (with the addition of a new back portion) on a busy downtown boulevard, Gehry's building is a huge, entirely new-build, mixed-use structure on an imposing public open space. But in fact there are many similarities between the two buildings. Both are designed around central atria surmounted with glass roofs and both buildings are dominated by a sculptural, organic form which invades the heart of the structure like some amoebic bacteria spreading through the orthogonal rigidity which otherwise characterises the buildings.

Like the ING Bank in Budapest, Gehry's DG Bank is on a very sensitive site, a critical location from the points of view of history and urbanism. Both architects have used the dramatic effect of the contrast between a theatrically organic internal element and sober, urban elevations designed within strict planning guidelines. The stepped-back massing of the DG Bank's Behrenstrasse facade recalls the pioneering designs of Henri Sauvage in Paris and the visionary drawings of Antonio Sant'Elia. The facade is clad in a buff-coloured limestone matching the material of the Brandenburg Gate itself in an attempt to knit the structure into the historical fabric of the city centre. Each elevation is related to its specific context; the monumental massing of the Behrenstrasse facade is totally different to the simple elevation of the Pariser Platz elevation. This consists of an almost flush surface, perforated with austere punched openings, which contrasts dramatically with the many elaborate, classicising facades being built elsewhere on the square.

On entry to the building the visitor is confronted with views to the huge central atrium with its curving glass roof and floor. From the entrance lobby a timber-sheathed arcade leads to the building's elevator lobbies and the offices situated on either side of the atrium. The size of the central atrium and the expansive glass roof which covers it allow natural light into offices deep in the heart of the building. The interior of the building is almost overpowered by the looming, darkly threatening, form of the shell housing the main conference hall. Visible throughout the building, this stainless steel-clad monster subverts the otherwise conventional architectural mass of the bank. The extensive framework which gives structure to the glass roof and floor appears like a complex cage or net which is bulging and struggling to contain this curious organic form floating in the middle of the structure. The interior of this element is clad in timber, enriching the organic metaphor and creating a soft, almost womb-like space. Its billowing, curving shape produces an atmosphere which is less rigidly confrontational

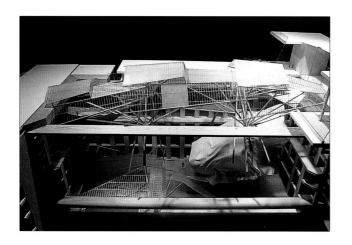

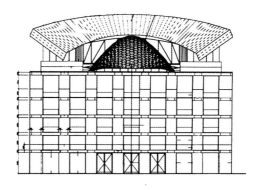

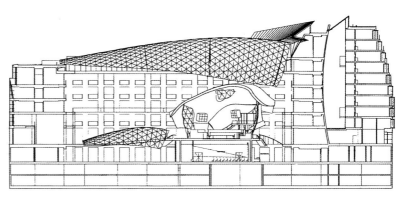

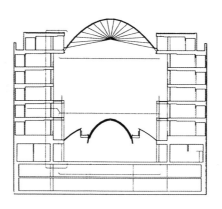

DG Bank, *Berlin*

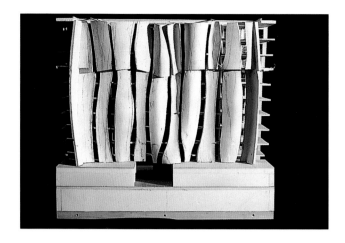

than the traditional meeting place in the bank while the curving seating and tables produce a more democratic layout than the more hierarchical rectangular setting. Beneath the organic shell is another smaller conference room which can be opened up into a larger space when combined with the neighbouring internal café space, a flexible volume capable of housing large receptions and banquets. The café is located beneath the curved glass vault which bulges up in front of the main conference space and thus receives plentiful light from the glass roof directly above.

The taller residential element of the building acts in section like a containing wall to stop the spread of the amoeboid conference room. The stepping back of the facade acts to reduce the volume of the building to the Behrenstrasse and creates terraces on the upper levels. The initial design was characterised by a pulsating, bulging series of curved bays which echoed the random, organic nature of the conference room within. This design was toned down to the final, more rational version which makes the contrast between the interior and the exterior all the more striking.

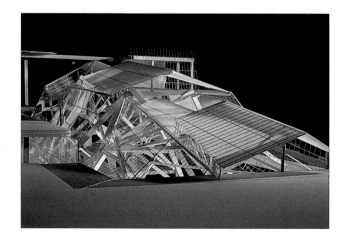

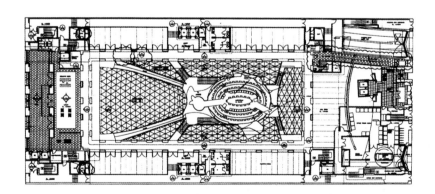

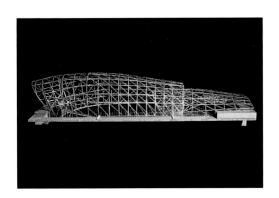

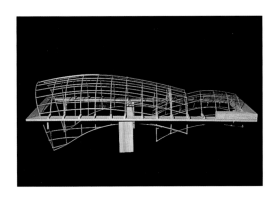

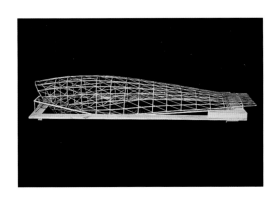

DG Bank, Berlin

KOHN PEDERSON FOX

Kohn Pederson Fox is one of the architectural practices most associated with the revival of the skyscraper as a building type. With the spread of the skyscraper beyond the shores of the USA, KPF has exerted an often monumental effect on cities all over the world. Certainly one of the most important and influential bank buildings to be erected during recent years in Europe, where the skyscraper is yet to be fully accepted as a part of the traditional cityscape, has been KPF's DG Bank in Frankfurt (1986-93).

Situated in a poorly defined and characterless area on the outskirts of the city centre of Frankfurt, the architects have attempted to create a self-contained complex which, despite its self-reliance, creates a sculptural and varied environment at street level. A composition of distinct elements creates a kind of mini, variegated urban townscape. The building is divided into three main elements: a glass-clad, curved office tower which is the tallest part of the building; a much lower perimeter building containing the building's residential element; and a central winter garden which acts as an atrium tying the other elements

together yet also reads as a distinct element within the composition. The architects play a rhythmic game of alternation between solid and void, stone and glass cladding, which successfully breaks down the mass of this huge complex. The tower element is itself composed of two distinct blocks which climb above the growing Frankfurt skyline in a structural embrace. A slender, rectangular block clad in stone rises through most of the building's height but it is overtaken at the top by the curved glazing of its sister tower. This culminates in a striking cantilevered crown echoing the 'DG' shape which is the corporate logo of the

DG Bank but also, more enigmatically, recalls the crown of the Statue of Liberty, the very symbol of the USA, a monument exported from Europe. In return Europe gets the skyscraper from the States.

DG Bank, *Frankfurt, 1986-93*

The European Headquarters for Goldman Sachs in Peterborough Court, London (1987-91), represents another intervention into the context of a European city centre but it is approached in an altogether different manner. The building is located on Fleet Street, the historic former centre of the news-paper industry, a real city centre site as opposed to the less defined Frankfurt site for the DG Bank. The situation demanded a more sensitive response and the building preserves the impressively monumental front of the old Daily Telegraph Building on the site. Compared to the typical London piecemeal development of this area, the new building is a monolithically huge structure, although the architects have attempted to reduce its impact on the surroundings and on the tight network of streets in a number of ways. The first of these is by reinstating Peterborough Court as a new courtyard between the old Telegraph Building and the large, new element thus separating and clearly demarcating the line between old and new but also pushing back the mass of the new building to reduce the impact of its height on the important thoroughfare of Fleet Street. The main building is a stone-clad symmetrical block with a large concave indent carved into it and is crowned by a shallow vaulted roof. The reception area, housed in a semi-circular plan, is located at the heart of the building and reached via a dramatic glazed gallery which tapers into a thin wedge. The curved walls of the lobby help to address the symmetries of the site rather in the manner of a Baroque spatial

sequence, the grand stair to the lift lobby springing off theatrically to one side.

Goldman Sachs, London, 1987-91

Thames Court, RABO Bank, *London, 1996-98*

Thames Court (1996-98) on the banks of London's river (now occupied by RABO Bank) is a particularly successful intervention into the heart of an established city centre. The building's height was kept low to comply with the regulations concerning the views of the dome of St Paul's Cathedral and it is to the benefit of the architecture; the restrictions and dimensions of the site impose a sleek, low shape which is emphasised by the elegant lightness of the riverside elevation. The elevation to the street is a deliberately heavier affair, its stone portal and the glass zone it frames creating a buffer to the noise of the busy street but maintaining the building's transparency. The building is organised around a series of attenuated multi-storey spaces and atria which maintain the same level of transparency and lightness within the building as the great expanses of glass suggest on the exterior.

World Bank Headquarters, *Washington DC, 1989-97*

The World Bank Headquarters in Washington DC (1989-97) is another low-rise building in another city which has shunned the skyscraper upon which KPF has built its reputation. The new building successfully takes its cue from the World Bank's two existing 1960s buildings which flank it. The new building is based around an expansive central space, top lit and airy, surmounted by a great vaulted roof reminiscent of a High-Tech railway station. The architectural language is light and transparent, a deliberate contrast to the solid construction which dominates the streets of the American capital; this is in part a deliberate series of architectural gestures to suggest penetrability and illumination, gestures attempting to counter-act notions of unaccountability and bureaucratic secrecy. It is an unusual departure from the more traditional language of solidity and security which has tended to define bank architecture since the collapse of International Style Modernism as the universal corporate architectural language.

The Federal Reserve Bank of Dallas (1989-92) is another relatively low building, the character of which is formed by the relationship of three distinct elements bound together by a central courtyard. The dominant element of the composition is an office tower supported on piloti which is bounded on the courtyard side by a huge blank wall. This terminates on the public side of the building in a pointed prow shape which gives the appearance of a single, immensely thick wall from which the offices are suspended. This component is skewed to the rest of the scheme which forms an L-shape on plan to create an irregular courtyard space at the centre. The walls framing the courtyard are treated as a gigantic abstract sculpture, the elements within the building being indicated by oversized openings, terraces or by repetitive grids of windows. The most striking feature is a giant glazed cube which sits proud of the building block behind it casting deep shadows on to the wall. This enormous opening illuminates the dining hall and starts to bring some of the openness of the courtyard into the interior of the building in a single grand gesture. A terrace to the side of the dining hall is sheltered from the sun by a deep cantilevered canopy which similarly casts oblique shadows on the stark walls of the bank adding to the quality of abstract composition and introducing an almost Suprematist aesthetic of geometric volumes floating in space.

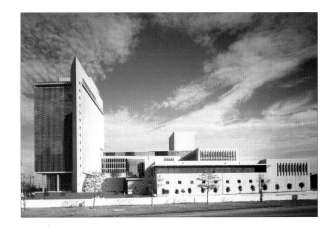

The headquarters building for the Bank Niaga, Jakarta, Indonesia (1989-93), like the Federal Reserve Bank in Dallas, is an attempt to create a self-sufficient environment, a microcosmic city and even encompasses a mosque on the site. The complex is dominated by a simple modern slab of an office block clad in stone, although the part of the building facing the more public realm of the city centre displays an aluminium curtain wall. The effort in the design seems to have gone towards mitigating the effects of the harsh sunlight; the windows of the ground-hugging parts of the building feature deep sun-screens and aluminium shelves which create a more pleasant environment at ground level.

OPPOSITE: **Federal Reserve Bank,** Dallas, 1989-92
ABOVE: **Bank Niaga,** Jakarta, 1989-93

In contrast, the Mellon Bank Center in Philadelphia (1984-90) is a skyscraper in the traditional East Coast mode, a solid, imposing mass which builds on the legacies of both Art Deco and Post-Modernism. The building played an instrumental role in the regeneration of Philadelphia and its rebirth as a financial centre, a position which it had been steadily losing since the halcyon days of the Philadelphia Savings Fund Society Building. Unlike the PSFS Building, a pioneering example of the emergent International Style and the first truly Modernist skyscraper, the Mellon Bank Center is a conservative, even Classical pile. Its form was inspired by an obelisk; the building's crown reveals its provenance, a gleaming pyramidal prism slightly reminiscent of IM Pei's Louvre pyramid, particularly at night when it is illuminated from within and its glazing allows a dazzling light to escape from the building's peak. The tower sits on a solid five-storey, stone-clad podium which roots it into the urban grid and context. A transitional phase between base and shaft, a few storeys of stone-clad block set back from the podium, creates the launching pad for the tapered tower. The tower itself is clad in gleaming aluminium which, like the glazing, dazzlingly reflects the sun when it is shining and the grey of the sky when it is dull. The grand entrance hall is clad in extravagantly veined marbles with details and lighting picked out in chrome-plated metal which adds to the nostalgic Art Deco atmosphere.

Mellon Bank Center, *Philadelphia, 1984-90*

The First Hawaiian Center, Honolulu, Hawaii (1991-95) is a more streamlined, modern version of the skyscraper type. The sleek tower is formed by the juxtaposition of a pair of contrasting elements, each characterised by its fenestration. One side of the tower gives views towards the sea and its elevation is composed of horizontally banded windows as part of a curtain-wall facade. The windows themselves are protected with horizontal louvres which further emphasise the directionality of the elevation. The other side of the tower gives views on to the island's mountains and, correspondingly, it is characterised by an architectural emphasis on the vertical. These two elements taper on plan and are placed next to each other to form an arrowhead shape upon a low level podium which contains a museum and the building's banking hall. The podium adjusts itself to the street plan and also helps define the borders to a series of gardens which encircle the building and soften its impact on the surroundings. The most striking aspect of the podium building is a large wall of prismatic-glass louvres which forms one of the walls of the banking hall and the museum. When natural light passes through the glass it creates what the architects have termed a 'kaleidoscopic' display of brilliant light which affects the mood, colour and brilliance of the interior to create a constantly changing spectral atmosphere.

First Hawaiian Center, Honolulu, 1991-95

KISHO KUROKAWA

Kisho Kurokawa's headquarters building for the Fukuoka Bank in Fukuoka (1971-75) is the oldest building included in this section but it is unusual and interesting enough to merit inclusion despite its age. The building is based around a generous gesture towards the public realm and in the atmosphere of Japan's notoriously overdeveloped city centres this gesture has great significance. A volume is subtracted from the main volume of the building which then wraps itself around the hole at its centre. That this is a missing volume (as opposed to merely an L-shaped building) is made clear by the massive column which defines one corner of the site and the roof which covers the open space nine floors above. Kurokawa's intention was to avoid the Western notion of the plaza as an entirely open space (a park or a square) but rather to create a place which embraces the traditional Japanese idea of an intermediate, semi-public space outside the building which dispenses with simple Western distinctions of outside and inside. He thus avoids the sense of nothingness which plagues many corporate Modernist buildings, where the windswept, empty plaza has come to represent everything that is most despised about the failures of the Modern Movement. The elevated urban space created within the boundaries of the site is modelled into a complex composition of terraces, steps, sculptures and benches and becomes an area where workers sit and chat, eat lunch and feel comfortable. If the development of the twentieth-century bank headquarters building can often be seen as an extension of billboard architecture – building as advertising hoarding for the financial institution – then Kurokawa's Fukuoka Bank created a precedent for an act of generosity towards the public realm and the city as well as its own customers and staff. This is a

OPPOSITE and ABOVE: **Fukuoka Bank**, *Fukuoka, 1971-75*

move which can become just as effective as a more obvious corporate statement expressed in expensive finishes or grand architectural gestures.

The section through the building shows that the notion of a complex space at the heart of the building governs the expansive subterranean areas of the bank as well as the defining plaza above. The area directly below the public space houses a large auditorium so that in the section the building's communal spaces coincide. The harsh stone and glass surfaces, which define the

bank building above ground, were deliberately designed so that the building would melt into its grey surroundings inconspicuously rather than drawing attention to its huge mass. The auditorium below, in contrast, is characterised by a richly organic brick shell which recalls the undulating work of Eladio Dieste in Mexico and earlier organic precedents by Gaudí and Rudolf Steiner. The subterranean quality of the space is emphasised by both the brick surfaces (a material returning to the earth) and the rough-hewn qualities of the

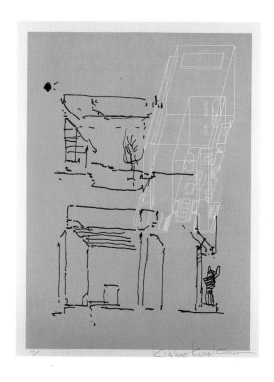

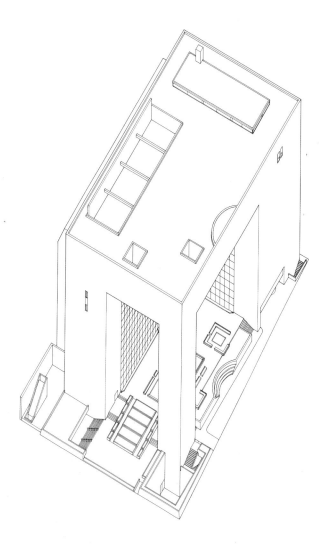

walls which seem to have been carved out of the ground. The building appears to have two poles: the cavernous auditorium and the artificial sky created by the overhanging structure. This canopy is studded with lights so that at night, on looking up, the visitor is struck by a kind of surrogate skyscape, the stars shining brilliantly illuminating a large Japanese horuto tree in the plaza which acts as a bridge between the worlds of above and below.

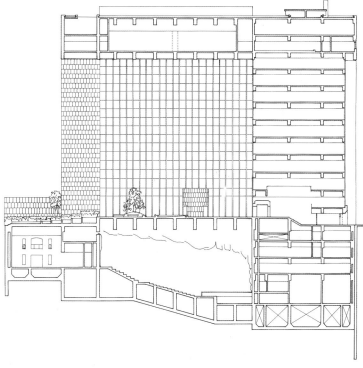

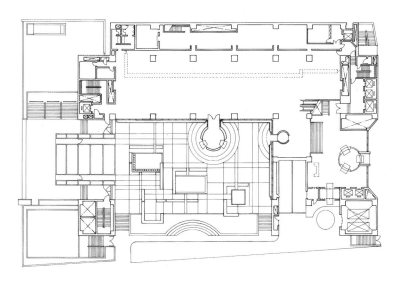

JOHN McASLAN AND PARTNERS

The Turkish bank, Yapi Kredi, is in the vanguard of technological innovation in the country's banking system. The rational and finely detailed Modernist structure designed by John McAslan and Partners to house its operations centre in Gebze, Turkey, reflects an embracing of technology and change as a fundamental tenet of modern banking. The operations centre houses a huge range of facilities including accommodation for the bank's main processing and data storage centres, its archives and its training and tele-banking centres. In addition the centre houses restaurants and cafes, sports facilities and a medical centre. It is rarely practical to position such large premises in city centres and, as would be expected, Yapi Kredi's operations centre is situated near the Istanbul to Ankara highway. As these facilities tend to be located away from city centres they tend to be architecturally unexciting; without the need to impress with an architectural display of bravado and status, the design of out-of-town operations centres tends towards the idiom of the tin-shed. But this scheme is an exception.

To the outside, the building presents a solid but self-effacing image, a long, stepped profile which clings to the side of a hill. The architects were throughout very conscious of the local building traditions and those of the broader world of Islam; not in a stylistic sense but in attempting to draw on the organisational traditions of a few building types. It is hard to imagine a more modern building type than the High-Tech bank operations centre yet perhaps it is this detachment which allowed the architects and the engineers (Ove Arup and Partners) to develop a solution

which successfully builds on a tradition without mimicking any specifics. The models are the ancient archetypes of the *caravanserai* and the bazaar, both building types which blend accommodation and trade, as well as social and commercial interaction. Both paradigms tend to be based on a modular system; these were buildings which could easily be expanded as trade grew and as the importance of the venue increased. As the buildings enlarged they tended to develop as self-contained cities growing around a series of internal streets and spaces within which the service industries began to appear to cater for the needs of the traders and

RIGHT and OPPOSITE: **Yapi Kredi Bank**, *Istanbul*

the customers. It is around this notion that the Yapi Kredi building is organised. The building consists of ten square blocks which recall the rational, modular plans of both Herman Hertzberger and Louis Kahn as well as more ancient archetypes. These contain the building's principal business accommodation between which a series of internal streets house the circulation and relaxation functions. This system creates a very clear, rational plan which is capable of expansion through the addition of new modules and was also developed as a safeguard against the earthquakes to which the area is prone. The rationale is that there is greater room for movement within the overall building of a series of interlinked but individual modules than there would be in a similarly sized monolithic structure.

Positioned at the junctions of the internal streets, cylindrical nodules house the vertical circulation and off these sprout bathrooms encased in glass blocks. Light is allowed to penetrate to all levels of the building via a comprehensive use of glass, in the form of blocks, frosted panels and floors and glazed roofs as well as large windows. But, as they would have been in the *caravanserai,* the internal streets are shaded with fabric stretched between the walls at the upper levels. A large tensile canopy also protrudes from the building to offer shade and shelter and announce the entrance across a bridge. Like the bazaar and *caravanserai*, the building reveals little from the outside. The glories of Middle-Eastern architecture tend to be revealed on the inside, a shaded courtyard or a screened and tiled social

room. Here it is the cylindrical tower ahead which reveals that the building branches off to all points from that initial entrance and the cool shaded triple-height streets which induce the visitor to explore the interior.

The cafés and restaurants scattered around the internal streets afford places of rest in the circulation areas which keep the building informal and friendly. The building's position on the side of a hill inspired the form of the building with a number of broad sets of steps at points within the circulation network and these give a grander, more urban feel to certain areas. Bridges crossing these stairs and a series of bright yellow awnings shading the upper spaces, as well as the sculptural cylindrical stairs give a lively dynamic to these long open spaces. Varied and abundant light is the defining feature of the interior of the building. Filtering through from every part of the building, even the dense modular blocks do not rely solely on the internal circulation system for light but are provided with small courtyards ensuring natural illumination at all points no matter how deep in the structure. The same consideration has been given to the internal climate which is partly regulated by a solar control system and a low-energy cooling system both of which help to even out the exigencies and extremes of the rural Turkish climate. The ability of the building to accommodate change and absorb new developments in banking was proved beyond doubt when two modular units were added to the structure immediately after building work had started.

Yapi Kredi Headquarters, *Istanbul*

Also illustrated here are the designs for the Yapi Kredi Headquarters Building in Istanbul. Inspired by Kevin Roche's Ford Foundation Building, the bank is based around a large atrium which rises through six floors accommodating a public lobby and will be used to display a part of the bank's extensive collection of Islamic art. The glass curtain walls become diaphanous veils exposing the whole of the building's interior. Secure accommodation is placed in the extensive basement while at the top of the building the roofscape is defined by a series of sculptural elements and a garden terrace.

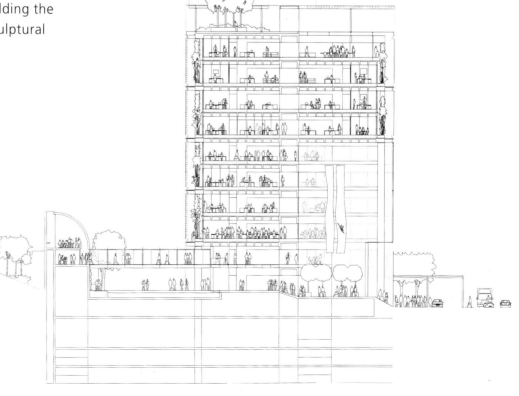

MEYER & VAN SCHOOTEN

The Dutch bank ING has had one of the most enlightened architectural commissioning policies of any bank in recent years. At the time of writing the most recent of these commissions is a new headquarters building for the ING Group in Amsterdam. Situated by the side of the motorway which encircles the city, this is a building with little urban context in the traditional sense, a situation which has left the architects free to play with the form of the building. Their solution is a streamlined building raised above the ground on converging stilt-like legs and the overall impression is that of the nose section of a high-speed train, an image which suits the constant speeding flow of the traffic by its side. The designs for the building dramatically illustrate the move towards openness and transparency which is emerging as a major trend in bank architecture. Traditionally, the bank has been seen as bastion; an impenetrable mass and this conception was only seriously challenged by the primacy of Modernism and the International Style from around the 1950s. The dawn of Post-Modernism towards the end of the 1970s saw a revived interest in solidity and the forms, or at least semiotic symbols and signs, of traditional architecture including the solid wall. The 1990s have seen a re-evaluation of the place of the Modernist vocabulary and, as in Meyer and

van Schooten's design, a kind of humanisation of the ideal. This new design incorporates features from both archetypal Modernist designs and Post-Modern and High-Tech innovations. The clarity of structure and the total transparency (peeling away the onion-skin layers of bureaucracy and inaccessibility) echo the work of Norman Foster, the idea of greened atria within the building also occurs within Foster's Commerzbank. The language, however, with its blend of super-modern and almost expressionistic devices is firmly rooted in the Dutch Modernist tradition, as is the attention to internal climate and the ingenious use of an aquaifer on site to assist with heating and cooling functions. Computer images alone are available at this point but they are enough to suggest an intriguing bank with which to commence the new century.

ING Group Headquarter Building, *Amsterdam*

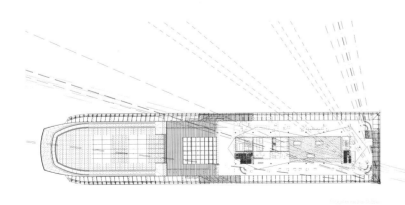

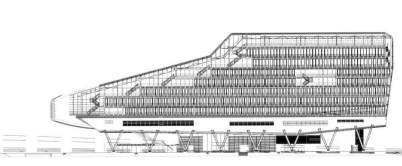

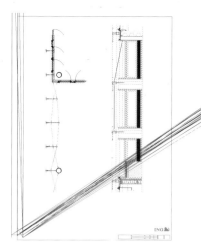

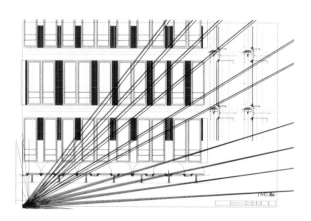

RAFAEL MONEO

The Bankinter building in Madrid (1972-77) is one of the oldest schemes featured in this section yet it is one of the buildings least tied to its age. The mass of brick and the monolithic yet self-effacing structure presaged the stark impressive mass of Moneo's magnificent Museum of Roman Art in Merida (1980-85) in which the architect emulated the stripped power of semi-ruined Roman structures, an approach which recalls JM Gandy's vision of Soane's Bank of England as a mass of ruins. Moneo's later Bank of Spain building in Jaén (1983-88) develops these themes further in its stark functionalism which derives less from the International Style of Functionalism familiar from banks all over the world than from a Mediterranean tradition of rationalism. In the vein of Gio Ponti or Giuseppe Terragni, these are modern, rational buildings with a historical tectonic context built into them. The Bankinter is placed next to a historic building in the Renaissance tradition with which it does not compete but rather acts as a foil. It presents a rigorous brick facade punched with a grid of square openings which, rather than being blank openings, are framed with a series of receding planes. These are the only modelling element in the depth of an otherwise flush brick elevation and they give an exaggerated impression of the depth of the walls reinforcing the notion that this is a strong-box of a building. Above the austerely flat facade two further storeys are accommodated within a different pattern of fenestration; four great openings give the effect of a penthouse arcade. Metal spandrels of vegetal decoration, reminiscent of those used by Louis Sullivan, are placed to cover the floor behind the openings. The division of the fenestration thus allows the top portion of the building with its different rhythm of solid and void to be perceived as a separate entity so reducing the apparent mass of the building and allowing it to harmonise with its smaller neighbours without overwhelming them.

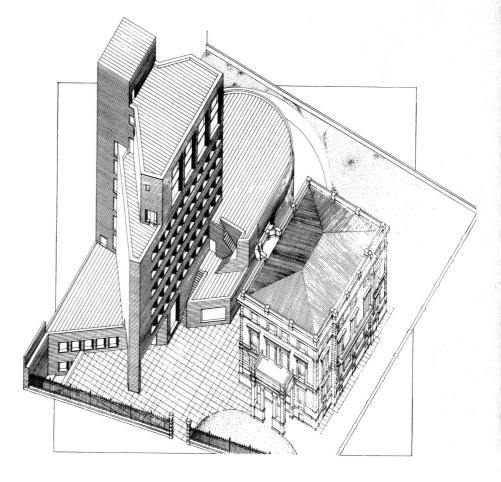

Bankinter, Madrid, 1972-77

At ground level a complex exercise in massing builds up a series of geometric volumes to create a sculptural intervention. A space is created in front of the building which allows the old building room to breathe and most of the volume at this level is distributed to the rear and the side of the site. The main component of the bank, however, a tapered element reminiscent of a ship's prow, impinges on the otherwise open forecourt through a single column at its corner which acts to provide a canopy and a natural opening for the building's main entrance without competing with the ornate door of its older neighbour. To the rear of the site the massing builds up to a two-storey structure which occupies a large part of the building's footprint and culminates in a broad curved block, the interior of which is illuminated by continuous bands of windows interrupted only by brick mullions which are rotated so that the corner presents itself to the facade and thus does not interrupt the continuity of the bands of glazing. A ramp wraps itself around this curve to provide access to the car park below. The building's interior is sparse and luxurious in a minimal fashion. High-quality polished stone is used throughout to provide continuous, smooth surfaces which reflect light from the irregular patterns of fenestration.

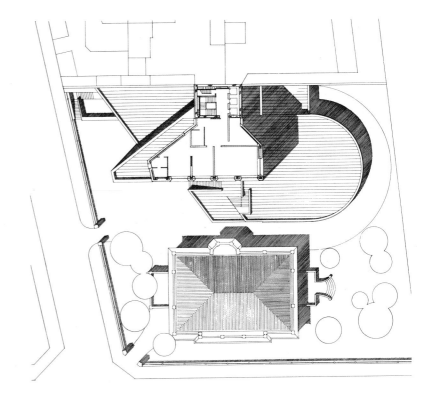

Bank of Spain, *Jaén*

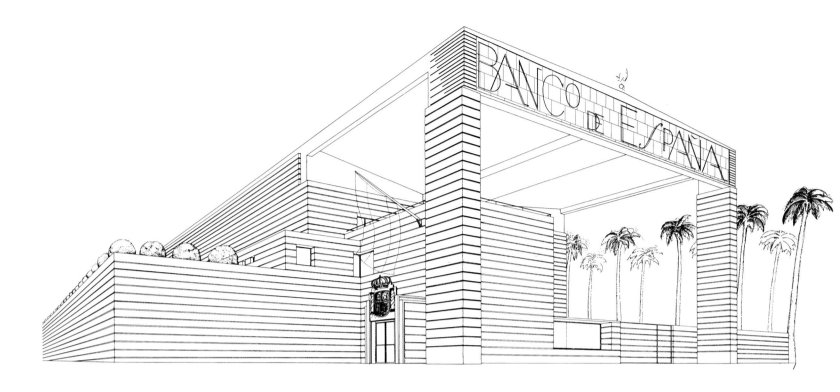

Bank of Spain, Jaén

The Bank of Spain Building in Jaén explores similar themes and can be seen as a continuation of the earlier building although the materials and articulation are ostensibly different. Here too Moneo sets up the bank building in a courtyard but here a canopy (rather than a cut-away) projects the building's presence more positively into the public realm. As at the Bankinter, the walls are expressed purely as powerful structural elements; oversized building blocks and deep mortar joints express the low horizontality of the building and give the impression of a fortified complex. By contrast the canopy projecting out on to the street is generous and open providing shade and shelter; it emphasises that, although secure, this is a public building. With this contrast Moneo addresses the question which has perplexed bank designers for centuries; the resolution of the paradoxical images of the bank as impenetrable to intruders yet neither intimidating nor repulsive. I think that in this building he is one of the very few architects to have solved this profound aesthetic and symbolic problem effectively. The building seems to have few openings on the ground floor. The main entrance (signified by a huge coat of arms above the door) is positioned beneath the canopy and to one side and the building is entered through a constrictive porch which gives the impression of thick walls. The main banking and office facilities are at higher levels entered via a long stair. The upper floor is illuminated on both sides by a continuous ribbon window. The fenestration reflects the plan intimately in the best Modernist tradition and the random (from the outside at least) puncturings create an interesting, rather medieval, appearance. The upper storey windows appear as a kind of loggia and this language is picked up again at the rear of the building. The building sits on the site like a remnant from Moorish times, yet is paradoxically modern; it exhibits impressive strength and bulk yet remains an addition to the urban realm which is on an intimately human scale in both its mass and materials. It is the perfect antidote to the glass tower.

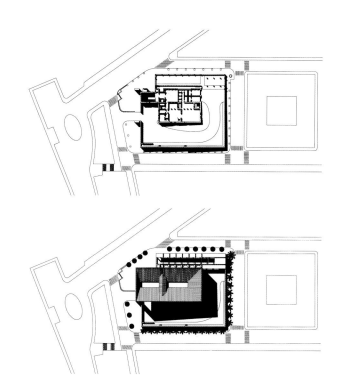

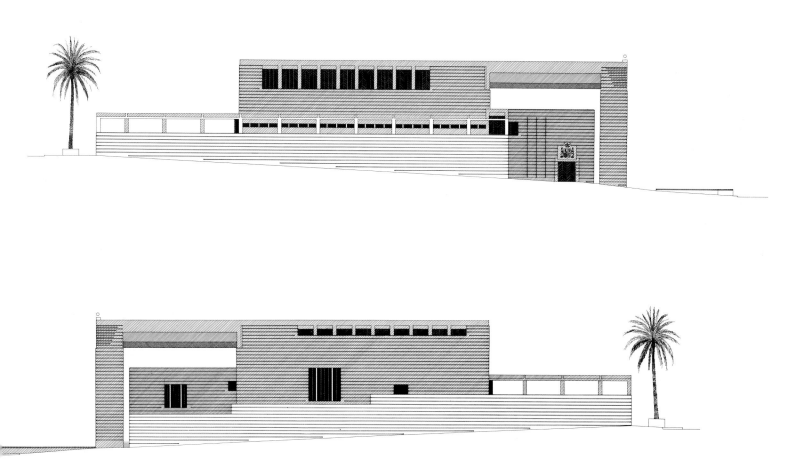

Bank of Spain, Jaén

MURPHY/JAHN

Bound into a tight urban site, the Savings of America Tower (1989-91) soars up into Chicago's dramatic skyline. A solid, rusticated base anchors the building into its urban context and the eye is drawn to a great curved hood above the entrance decorated with a mosaic mural by Roger Brown. Above this, the curve is taken up by a bay which rises through the full height of the building and subtly models the slender, attenuated facade. The curve of the bay also helps to focus attention on the small mid-block pedestrian link, leading towards Chicago's City Hall, which separates the building from its neighbour. This is further accentuated by a bulky pierced canopy which protrudes above the LaSalle Street sidewalk. The curved glass bay is terminated on one side by a ladder-like structure which shoots up beyond the top of the

bay becoming a solid wall at the crown of the building. Here it meets the swooping curve which defines the building's impact on the skyline. The top of the building is softened by this vaulted crown, its effect is less harsh than that of the Miesian skyscrapers which dominate the city's upper reaches (examples of which can be seen in the background of the photos). Rational yet thoughtful, the building fits well into the self-deprecating and workman-like tradition of Chicago's tough urban architecture. Banded and rusticated stone weigh it down while the delicate glass and curves echo the desire for ascent which is expressed in the Icarus mural at street level. The Icarus myth also serves as a cautionary tale against the arrogance of mankind, a subtle and rare reminder of mortality and fallibility in the world of banking.

OPPOSITE and ABOVE: **Savings of America Tower**, *Chicago, 1989-91*

The Barnett Center, for the Barnett Bank in Jacksonville, Florida, represents an altogether different approach. Its sculptural form is familiar from Helmut Jahn's expressive drawings which recall the confidence of the skyscraper builders of the Art Deco era. The building, like many of the great Art Deco works, was inspired by a monument of the ancients, in this case an obelisk. The ground floor houses both retail accommodation and a great banking hall, access to which is gained via a landscaped plaza. The building rises through forty-two floors and its sleek shell is clad in blue-grey granite and capped with a pyramidal crown creating a prominent and recognisable identity for the bank on the Jacksonville skyline. The building is a fine example of architecture creating a corporate symbol. The visually powerful and distinctive shape of the tower creates a local image for the bank, the institution becomes recognisable and is engrained in the local consciousness – architecture as advertising.

OPPOSITE and ABOVE: **Barnett Center**, *Jacksonville, Florida*

The Generale Bank Tower in Rotterdam, The Netherlands, makes an even more striking impression on the skyline. Built on an awkward site, the context of which incorporates historic local architecture, large modern office and apartment blocks, docks and canals, the architects have attempted to create a series of different buildings within one structure to address the various urban situations. Towards the historic Schielandhuisan an urban square is created, part of which is under the building, defined by huge trusses and columns. In this there are parallels with Kisho Kurokawa's cutaway corner at the Fukuoka Bank. The elevation of this part of the building on stilts allows views through to the Generale Bank's historic neighbour. It constitutes an urban gesture which acknowledges that the new building will inevitably overwhelm its neighbours but, at least, parts of them will remain visible. It ends up as a kind of framing device which works surprisingly well. The columns which define the edge of this plaza flare out towards the top and begin to announce the facade which continues to slant dramatically outwards throughout its full height. This angled element is juxtaposed with the taller part of the structure which is clad in stone and thus differentiated. This bulky element changes character almost schizophrenically from elevation to elevation. Towards the historic part of the town it presents a facade characterised by a stepped, projecting element against a flat elevation which rises above the roof and which culminates in a cut-out square revealing the sky beyond. Its counterpart above the stepped projection is the bank's name in huge letters. The other side of the building reveals a broad sweeping curve throughout the height of the structure. This is terminated by a grating suspended on bracing at the top of the building which casts a grid of shadows on to the recessed top floors.

OPPOSITE and ABOVE: **Generale Bank Tower**, *Rotterdam*

MURRAY O'LAOIRE

The Stolichny Bank Building (1990), designed by Irish architects Murray O'Laoire on the banks of the Vodootvodny Canal was one of the first new buildings in Moscow after the collapse of the Communist regime. The planning authorities demanded the retention of an unassuming existing facade on the site, an elevation which had formerly fronted a derelict building. The retention and incorporation of the old building and the size of the accommodation required for the new bank building necessitated an arrangement consisting of a kind of progressive piling up of architectural elements. The pile culminates in a glazed strip which runs along the highest point of the building, parallel to the canal. This element, capped by a curving glazed roof, illuminates an atrium which rises through the full height of the

building. Also parallel to the canal, this effectively splits the structure into two office blocks. The light from the glazed roof is regulated by a series of curved mechanical louvres which deflect light down on to a series of metal sculptural elements suspended in the air within the central atrium space.

The building is entered through a vaulted passage from the retained and restored elevation. From here the visitor arrives at a lobby where a glimpse is given of the entire height of the converted building (with its floors removed) and this then opens on to the full-height five-storey atrium. The bank's circulation is confined to the areas at either end of this central corridor and the two blocks are linked by gangway bridges across the atrium.

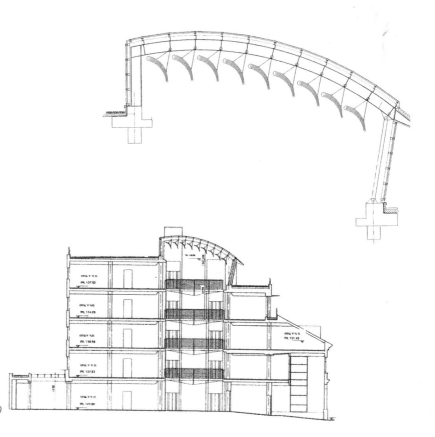

OPPOSITE and ABOVE: **Stolichny Bank Building**, *Moscow 1990*

NIKKEN SEKKEI

The slim plan of the headquarters building of the Long Term Credit Bank of Japan in Tokyo (completed in 1993) was determined by a tightly confined strip site in the city's Hibiya district. Nikken Sekkei addressed the confinement around the bank's base by designing a building with a T-shaped section which only expands to its full width eight storeys above street level. This kinking back of the lower levels allows the creation of a plaza to either side of the base. In the same way in which Kisho Kurokawa's Fukuoka Bank blurs traditional Western architectural notions of inside and outside, so Nikken Sekkei's solution attempts a similar feat. The plaza from which the bank is entered is paved in marble and even the trees have a hard, regular look (compounded by metal containing cages around their bases). Bollards, lighting and other metal street furniture set up a harsh, man-made, meticulously assembled aesthetic that runs right through into the hard, grey marble paving stones which make up the floor of the entrance lobby. A vast wall of glass diminishes the barriers between the plaza and the lobby although entry is emphasised by a small lobby set outside the building and exists as an almost autonomous element. The entrance lobby is surrounded on three sides by completely glazed walls which rise through four huge storeys. The roof also is fully glazed and the soffit of the cantilevered building above is barely visible and yet exerts its presence in the ominous shadow it casts on the fully glazed box below.

To either side of the asymmetrically placed doors completely glazed lift shafts appear like mere ghosts of structure and these bring people up from the extensive car-parking set below the building so that all visitors enter at the great glass wall. The glass lift-shafts appear as see-through booths bringing visitors up only as far as the ground floor. From there, escalators, which are also placed asymmetrically within the vast lobby space, convey visitors up to the main banking hall on the first floor. The escalators penetrate an opening in a wall which announces the beginning of the building proper. A curved wall funnels visitors into the long, attenuated banking hall which is terminated by another wall of glass at the far end of the building, this time in a grid of

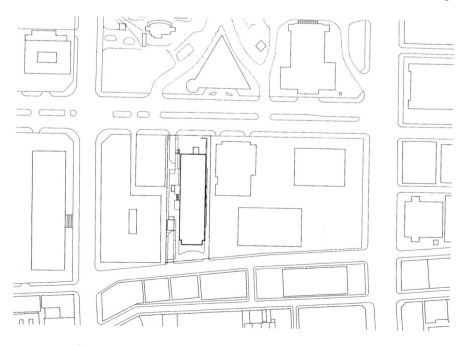

Long Term Credit Bank of Japan, Tokyo, 1993

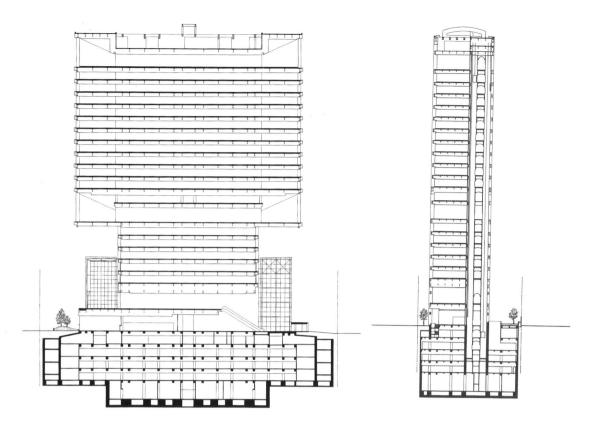

frosted glass reminiscent of the paper screens of traditional Japanese architecture. Beyond this screen wall stands another of the impressive single-space glass boxes which greeted the visitor at the beginning of the route through the bank. This space looks out on to a small landscaped garden which balances the plaza at the front of the building. Above the banking hall the shaft of the structure is occupied by office space and as the building flares out the cantilevered corners are occupied by double-height spaces housing a tea-room, cafeteria and large canteen. These double-height spaces are expressed on the elevations with massive picture windows as are the double-height spaces on the top floor which contain rooms for receptions and conferences.

The bank's super-frame structure, which includes a computer controlled anti-seismic system, is clearly visible on the side elevations where triangular trusses appear both at the bottom and the top of the broader section of the building.

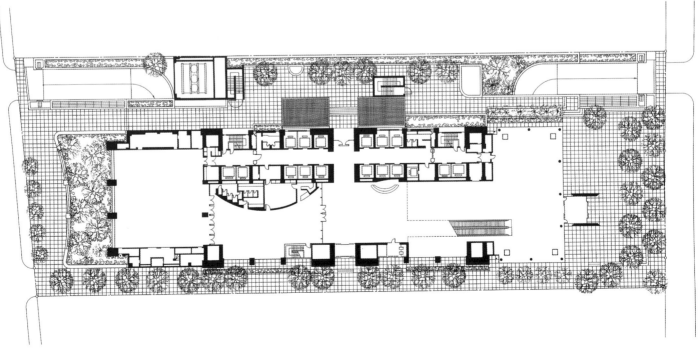

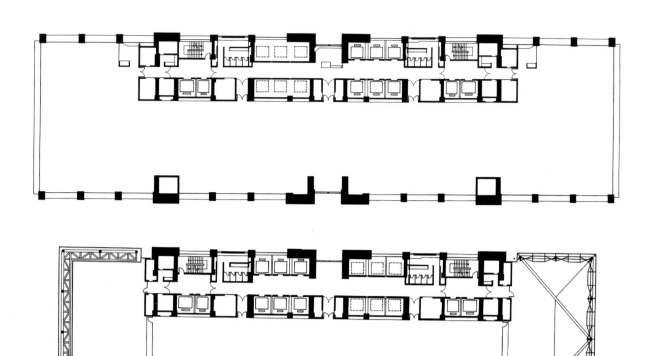

CESAR PELLI

Cesar Pelli is one of the architects most associated with the renaissance of the skyscraper as an iconic building form with its own mode of tectonic expression, an expression which looks back fondly to the extravagances of the Art Deco era. For the mid twentieth century the skyscraper as a building type became a vertically extended version of the Miesian glass box which dominated corporate and business architecture in the Western world and subsequently in the rest of the world as the corporations spread their tentacles. The revival of sculptural expression and of the forms of the 1930s dates essentially from the 1980s and the massive expansion of the markets and the wealth, influence and confidence of the banks. The monumental skyscraper is the architectural expression of that growing confidence and the renewed longing for architecture to function once again as corporate symbol; for the head-quarters building to make its presence felt in the urban context and on the skyline. The Norwest Center, Minneapolis, Minnesota (1985-89), is a reflection of the extent of the return to the 1930s aesthetic. The slender skyscraper with its complex stepped top is reminiscent of the visionary drawings of Hugh Ferris which defined the sky-scraper aesthetic in the 1920s and 1930s. Even the attenuated piers at street level, the geometric relief decoration and the large, monumental opening recall the Art Deco age.

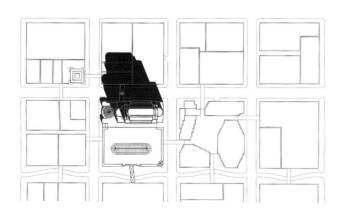

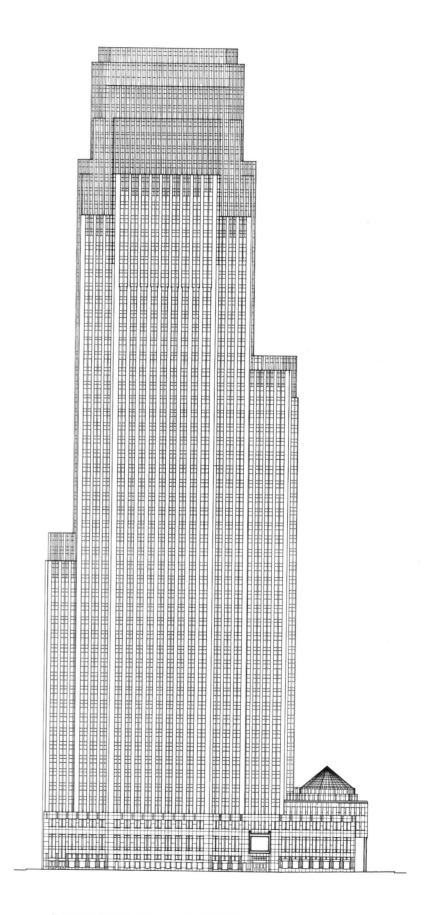

Norwest Center, *Minneapolis, 1985-89*

OPPOSITE:**Nations Bank Corporate Center**, *Charlotte, 1987-92*

The Nations Bank Corporate Center, Charlotte, North Carolina (1987-92), also recalls the golden age of the tall building with a dramatic, gleaming metallic crest. An intricate series of steel spikes arranged in curved banks produces a literal crown effect at the top of the building. At ground level the building houses a complex which comprises almost an entire city in itself. It includes a performing arts centre as well as public restaurant, retail and health club facilities. A public plaza is also created and bounded by a wavy water-feature which has the effect of isolating the square from the street and the traffic while leaving it accessible and open.

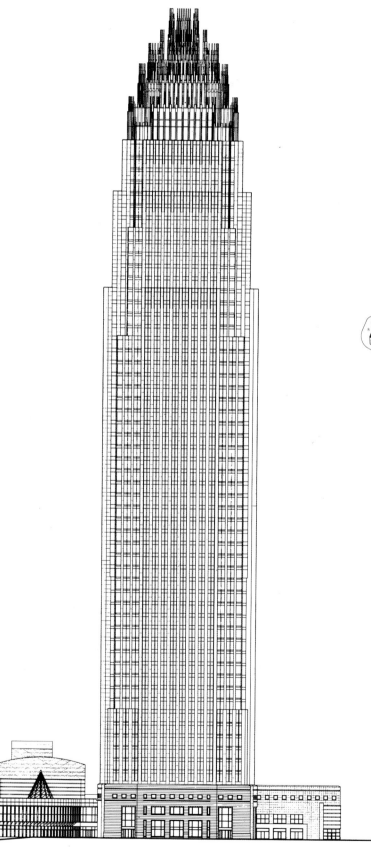

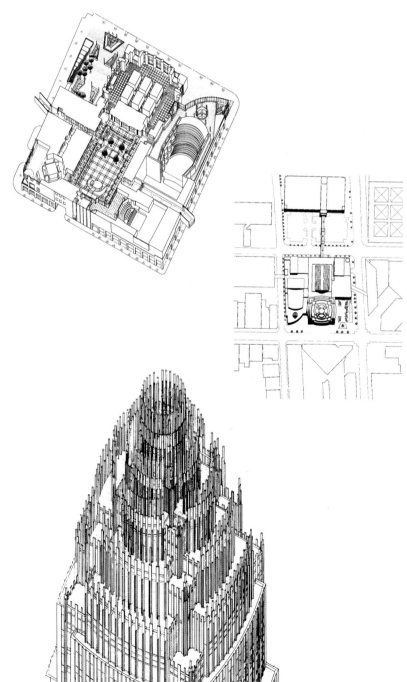

Society Center, Cleveland, 1987-92

Society Center, Cleveland, Ohio (1987-92), also prominently displays a pyramidal, stainless-steel, Deco-influenced crown which can be seen most clearly when illuminated at night. This scheme also involved the restoration of Burnham and Root's 1889 Society for Savings Bank, the banking hall of which featured impressive murals by Walter Crane.

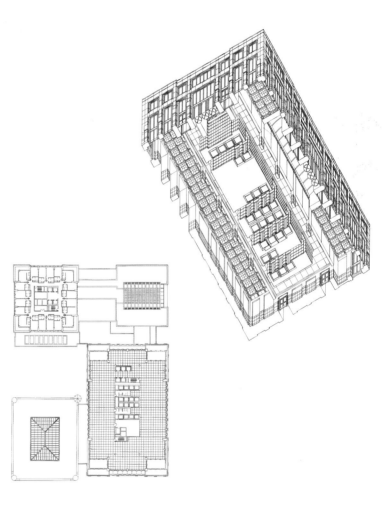

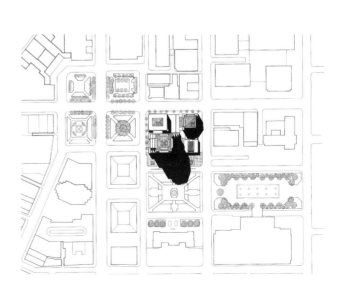

The Wachovia Center, Winston-Salem, North Carolina (1993-95), features a domed crown which recalls the shape of an observatory rather than that of the Art Deco buildings which so obviously influenced many of Pelli's famous skyscrapers. The square plan of the building at street level goes through a sequence of progressively larger chamfers as it rises until the plan of the top storeys becomes an octagon, preparing the way for a smoother transition to the domed form of the top of the skyscraper. The building is set behind a large landscaped garden at the centre of which an oval plaza is created. The entrance is never arrived at directly, but always via a pattern of swirling paths and wavy routes. Luxurious interiors in brown, white and black stone give an air of opulence and 1930s' grandeur to this otherwise rather austerely white design. The office is currently working on the

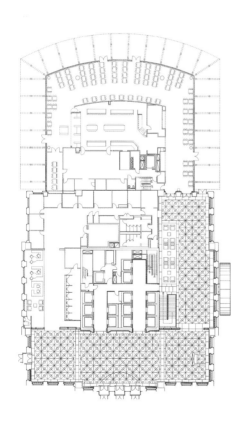

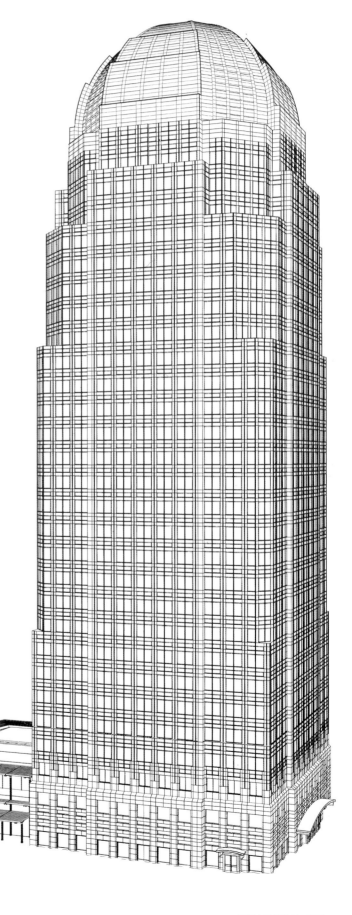

Wachovia Center, *Winston-Salem, 1993-95*

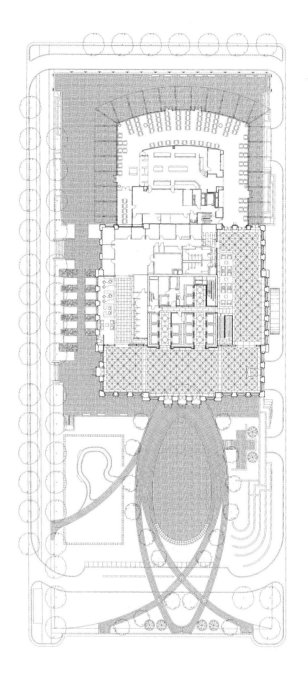

OPPOSITE: **Torre Bank Boston**, *Buenos Aires*

designs for Torre Bank Boston in Buenos Aires, Argentina (1997-2000). Situated in a tightly controlled city-centre location, the building was subject to very tight planning restrictions on its appearance and profile which partly explains the departure from Pelli's more flamboyantly Post-Modern approach. The identity of this building is determined by the prismatic profile of its crown which results from a series of angled set-backs starting half way up the building.

GMP: VON GERKAN, MARG AND PARTNER

In the wake of the reunification of Germany, the heart of pre-war Berlin, the Pariser Platz, has again become the focus of interest in a scheme to reinstate this pivotal square as the hub of the city. At the termination of Unter den Linden, Berlin's main axial avenue, stands the Brandenburg Gate and beyond this, the Pariser Platz. The historical and urban significance of the site haze prompted the city authorities to employ a virtually unprecedented degree of control over the architecture and planning of this still sensitive central place. The rigorous regulations have led to a public space which is a little blank, cold, formal and controlled, exhibiting the stiff self-restraint of a city still hesitant in its approach to the rebuilding of its monumental set-pieces. Thus the facades to the square are largely self-deprecating, modest but tentatively Classical efforts, trying hard to be inoffensive to all. The interior of Frank Gehry's DG Bank erupts into a flowing blob, an ebullient organic form trying to escape the rigours of the elevation. Meinhard Von Gerkan's Dresdner Bank (1995-97) also creates an internalised, inward-looking world to counter the strict planning controls on the facades.

The bank is built around a huge hole at its centre. The atrium, which has become a feature of so many modern office buildings, here represents the heart of the structure rather than the bland light-well which it often becomes. The plan looks more like that of a theatre than a bank, with small, individual offices clustered around a huge central auditorium like boxes at the opera. But the architectural expression of the atrium is reminiscent of one of the historic archetypes of bank and exchange architecture, which derives from the archaic central courtyard model. Its precedents can be seen at Soane's Rotunda in the Bank of England and Lecamus de Mézières' Halle au Blé in Paris. But its steel and glass interior recalls much more strongly the industrial aesthetic of J B Bunning's London Coal Exchange and Cuthbert Broderick's Leeds Corn Exchange from the middle of the nineteenth century. Like these buildings, the Dresdner Bank is built up around a drum-like central court crowned with a shallow glass dome, illuminated from the central space from which the plan radiates. While the earlier buildings had a series of cast iron galleries, the Dresdner Bank has a series of window cleaning

Dresdner Bank, in context showing Pariser Platz and the Brandenburg Gate

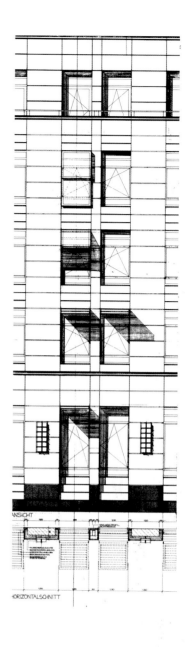

Dresdner Bank, *1995-97*

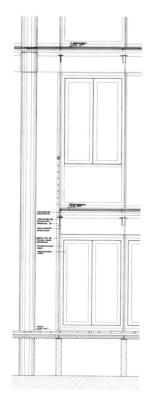

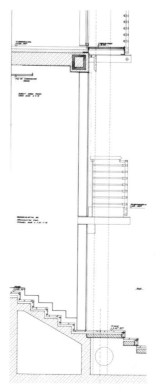

balconies running continuously around the perimeter of the cylindrical atrium. Each of these has a glass floor and the complex patterns of mullions, structural glazing bars, handrails and meshes builds up a hard industrial aesthetic which is at odds with the restrained, civil architecture of the facade. It is this contrast which gives the building its power; the surprise of the switch from the flat, blank stone of the elevation to the sculpted, metallic drum of the atrium. The industrial appearance of this central space is compounded by a cleaning gantry suspended from the glazed dome, the lifts within a simple tower of I-beams and a sculptural spiral stair all of which conspire to give an almost Constructivist revelling in the aesthetic of the factory. The interior architecture becomes a straightforward and honest tectonic metaphor: this is a factory for making money.

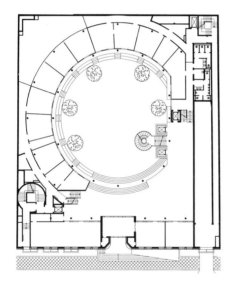

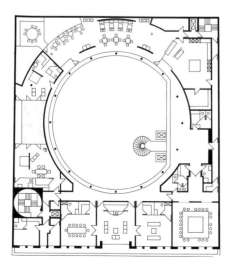

ABOVE: Ground floor plan
BOTTOM: Typical floor plan

WHINNEY MACKAY-LEWIS

The bank building pedigree of City of London office Whinney Mackay-Lewis dates back to the nineteenth century and in the twentieth century the practice worked in association with Edwin Lutyens on a number of bank buildings. Two of the buildings featured here, the Banque Paribas (1998) and Credit Suisse (1996) are among the largest recent bank buildings in London and, interestingly, both have been built outside the City of London, the traditional hub of the financial markets. Computerisation and deregulation of the markets have led to a redistribution of the banking centre. Although it remains firmly focused on the City, the formerly inconceivable act of building a major bank outside the City boundaries has become a frequently seen occurrence. The new London headquarters of the French Banque Paribas occupies an entire urban block in London's Marylebone. The building is based around a central atrium beneath a huge glazed dome which dominates the skyline. The influence of the curves of the dome is felt throughout the building from the semi-circular glass canopy which projects from the cylinder housing the main entrance to the semi-circular entrance lobby which creates a first atrium and the circular auditorium which sits in the centre of the ground floor directly beneath the dome.

The building's main elevation is centred around a dramatic glass facade, a sheer wall of glazing between the masonry walls. This represents the architects' attempt to knit the building into the surrounding urban fabric which includes Marylebone Station and a large Victorian hotel. The huge curving mullions (in effect bow-string trusses) of the glass facade and the suspended glass canopy are the architects' only real concession to grand architectural gesture. It was made clear by the Banque Paribas that this was not to

be a flagship corporate headquarters, this was achieved at their new Paris headquarters in Ricardo Bofill's market-hall type building, but a functional building housing the massive dealing and banking operations – what the architects term a 'dealer factory'. Despite the utilitarian connotations of this phrase, the rational approach does not mean that the architects have created a Dickensian factory floor. The bank is in fact saturated with natural light throughout, despite the depth of the office floors. Glass is used wherever possible and even the lift shafts are theatrically glazed so as not to disrupt the flow of light through the building. The lifts are surrounded by voids which travel through the full

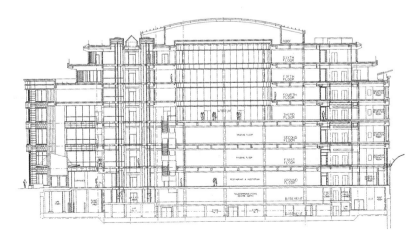

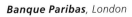

Banque Paribas, *London*

ABOVE: **Credit Suisse First,** *Boston*
BELOW: **Banque Paribas,** *London; plan*

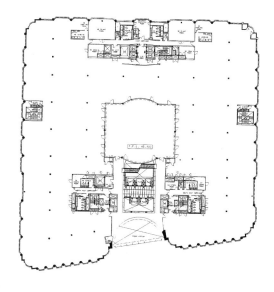

height of the building and which give a clear identity and sense of place within a deep plan which could otherwise disorient the user. The trading floors which dominate the plan are huge; uninterrupted flowing space dictated by the need for traders to maintain contact with their colleagues at all times. These are the factory floors of the building, inevitably overwhelming, the endless vista of computer screens and desks which can be seen in trading floors all over the world. It is left to the clean, crisp circulation spaces and the lobbies and atria to provide the architectural drama.

A building occupied by Royal and Sun Alliance in Berkeley Square (1997), the heart of London's Mayfair features a similarly conservative facade enlivened by a dramatic canopy featuring an art work created by the architects. Inside the crisp modern interiors are characterised by a mix of glass, stone and bronze which creates infinitely subtle variations in colour and shadow through-out the building.

OPPOSITE: **Banque Paribas**, London
RIGHT: **Royal and Sun Alliance**, London

Whinney Mackay-Lewis boast close cooperation with artists and many of the interiors of their buildings are planned either with certain works of art in mind or the artists are called in at an early stage to work with the architects. The restaurant area for Credit Suisse First Boston at One Cabot Square in London's Docklands is enlivened by the bright colours of Bruce Maclean's artwork (executed with a Matisse-like simplicity) while the staff restaurant of the London office of Banque Paribas features the work *Winging* by Adam Craig.

Banque Paribas, *London; restaurant*

BIBLIOGRAPHY AND SOURCES

Bakonyi, Tibor and Kubinszky, Mihály, *Lechner Ödön*, Corvina, Budapest 1981

Booker, John, *Temples of Mammon: The Architecture of Banking*, Edinburgh University Press, 1990

Borsi, Franco and Godoli, Ezio, *Vienna 1900: Architecture and Design*, Lund Humphries, London 1986

Brooks, H Allen, *The Prairie School: Frank Lloyd Wright and his Midwest Contemporaries*, University of Toronto Press 1972

Brooks, Michael W, *John Ruskin and Victorian Architecture*, Thames and Hudson, London 1989

Bush-Brown, Albert, *Louis Sullivan*, George Braziller Inc., New York 1960

Dixon, Roger and Muthesius, Stefan, *Victorian Architecture*, Thames and Hudson, London 1978

Dupre, Judith (introduction featuring Philip Johnson), *Skyscrapers*, Black Dog and Leventhal, New York 1996

Fessy, Georges (photographer), *Odile Decq and Benoit Cornette - Banque Populaire de l'Ouest*, Les Editions du Demi Cercle, Paris 1990

Geretsegger, Heinz and Peintner, Max, *Otto Wagner 1841-1918*, Academy Editions, London 1979

Gerle, Janos, *Palaces of Money*, City Hall, Budapest 1994

Goldberger, Paul, *The Skyscraper*, Allen Lane, Penguin Books, London 1982

Granell, Enrique (Editor), *Bankinter, 1972-1977 - Ramon Bescos, Rafael Moneo*, Colegio de Arqitectos de Almeria, Almeria 1994

Green, Edwin, *Banking: An Illustrated History*, Phaidon, London 1989

Kohlenbach, Bernhard, *Hendrik Petrus Berlage: Über Architektur und Stil*, Birkhäuser, Basel 1991

Moravánszky, Ákos, *Competing Visions: Aesthetic Invention and Social Imagination in Central European Architecture, 1867-1918*, MIT Press, Massachusetts 1998

Parissien, Steven (Ed), *Banking on Change, A Current Account of Britain's Historic Banks*, The Georgian Group, The Victorian Society, The Thirties Society and The Ancient Monuments Society, London 1992

Pevsner, Nikolaus, *A History of Building Types*, Thames and Hudson, London 1979

Roth, Leland M, *A Concise History of American Architecture*, Harper and Row, New York 1979

Roth, Leland M, *McKim, Mead and White Architects*, Thames and Hudson, London 1984

Rucker, Darnell, *The Chicago Pragmatists*, University of Minnesota Press, Minneapolis 1969

Schorske, Carl E, *Vienna 1900*, George Weidenfeld and Nicholson Ltd, London 1981 (first published 1961)

Schuyler, Montgomery, *American Architecture and Other Writings*, Athenium, New York 1963

Singelnberg, Peter, *H P Berlage: Idea and Style*, Haentjens Dekker and Gumbert, Utrecht 1972

Sullivan, Louis H, *Autobiography of an Idea*, Dover, New York 1954 (first published 1924)

Summerson, John, *Georgian London*, Barrie and Jenkins (revised edition), London 1988 (1st edition 1945)

Summerson, John and Watkin, David, *John Soane*, Academy Editions, London 1983

Summerson, John, *The Unromantic Castle and Other Essays*, Thames and Hudson, London 1990

Weingarden, Lauren S, *Louis H. Sullivan: The Banks*, MIT Press 1987

De Wit, Wim (Ed), *Louis Sullivan: The Function of Ornament*, Saint Louis Art Museum 1986

INDEX